MW01156584

Under Control

Governance Across the Enterprise

Jacob Lamm

*Sumner Blount, Steve Boston, Marc Camm, Robert Cirabisi,
Nancy E. Cooper, Dr. Galina Datskovsky, Ph.D., CRM,
Christopher Fox, Kenneth V. Handal, William E. McCracken,
John Meyer, Helge Scheil, Alan Srulowitz, Rob Zanella*

ca PRESS

Apress®

Under Control: Governance Across the Enterprise

Copyright © 2010 by CA, Inc., excepting Chapter 5, copyright © 2010 by William E. McCracken. All rights reserved. All trademarks, trade names, service marks and logos referenced herein belong to their respective companies.

The information in this publication could include typographical errors or technical inaccuracies, and the authors assume no responsibility for its accuracy or completeness. The statements and opinions expressed in this book are those of the authors and are not necessarily those of CA, Inc. ("CA"). CA may make modifications to any CA product, software program, method or procedure described in this publication at any time without notice.

Any reference in this publication to third-party products and websites is provided for convenience only and shall not serve as the authors' endorsement of such products or websites. Your use of such products, websites, any information regarding such products or any materials provided with such products or on such websites shall be at your own risk.

To the extent permitted by applicable law, the content of this book is provided "AS IS" without warranty of any kind, including, without limitation, any implied warranties of merchantability, fitness for a particular purpose, or non-infringement. In no event will the authors or CA be liable for any loss or damage, direct or indirect, arising from or related to the use of this book, including, without limitation, lost profits, lost investment, business interruption, goodwill or lost data, even if expressly advised in advance of the possibility of such damages. Neither the content of this book nor any software product referenced herein serves as a substitute for your compliance with any laws (including but not limited to any act, statute, regulation, rule, directive, standard, policy, administrative order, executive order, and so on (collectively, "Laws") referenced herein or otherwise. You should consult with competent legal counsel regarding any such Laws.

All rights reserved. No part of this work may be reproduced or transmitted in any form or by any means, electronic or mechanical, including photocopying, recording, or by any information storage or retrieval system, without the prior written permission of the copyright owner and the publisher.

ISBN-13 (pbk): 978-1-4302-1592-9

ISBN-13 (electronic): 978-1-4302-1593-6

Printed and bound in the United States of America 9 8 7 6 5 4 3 2 1

Trademarked names may appear in this book. Rather than use a trademark symbol with every occurrence of a trademarked name, we use the names only in an editorial fashion and to the benefit of the trademark owner, with no intention of infringement of the trademark.

President and Publisher: Paul Manning
Lead Editor: Jeffrey Pepper
Contributing Editor: Lynne Mahoney
Editorial Board: Clay Andres, Steve Anglin, Mark Beckner, Ewan Buckingham, Gary Cornell, Jonathan Gennick, Jonathan Hassell, Michelle Lowman, Matthew Moodie, Duncan Parkes, Jeffrey Pepper, Frank Pohlmann, Douglas Pundick, Ben Renow-Clarke, Dominic Shakeshaft, Matt Wade, Tom Welsh
Coordinating Editor: Jim Markham
Copy Editor: Tiffany Taylor
Compositor: Apress Production
Indexer: nSight, Inc.
Artist: April Milne
Cover Designer: Anna Ishchenko

Distributed to the book trade worldwide by Springer-Verlag New York, Inc., 233 Spring Street, 6th Floor, New York, NY 10013. Phone 1-800-SPRINGER, fax 201-348-4505, e-mail orders-ny@springer-sbm.com, or visit http://www.springeronline.com.

For information on translations, please contact Apress by e-mail info@apress.com, or visit http://www.apress.com.

Apress and friends of ED books may be purchased in bulk for academic, corporate, or promotional use. eBook versions and licenses are also available for most titles. For more information, reference our Special Bulk Sales–eBook Licensing web page at http://www.apress.com/info/bulksales.

The information in this book is distributed on an "as is" basis, without warranty. Although every precaution has been taken in the preparation of this work, neither the author(s) nor Apress shall have any liability to any person or entity with respect to any loss or damage caused or alleged to be caused directly or indirectly by the information contained in this work.

Contents

About the Authors...vi

Contributors xvii

Acknowledgments.. xviii

Introduction... xix

Chapter 1: The Rise of Governance
by Jacob Lamm... 1

Chapter 2: Governance Today
by Jacob Lamm.. 15

Chapter 3: Policy Management
by Sumner Blount 25

Chapter 4: Risk Management
by Sumner Blount 35

Chapter 5: Risk Governance and the Board of Directors
by William E. McCracken................................. 55

Chapter 6: Governance of Risk and Compliance
by Robert Cirabisi and Kenneth V. Handal 73

Chapter 7: **IT Governance, Risk, and Compliance**
by Rob Zanella 87

Chapter 8: **Governance and Portfolio Management**
by John Meyer and Helge Scheil 107

Chapter 9: **The Regulatory Environment**
by Marc Camm and Christopher Fox 123

Chapter 10: **Governance and Finance**
by Nancy E. Cooper and Alan Srulowitz...........................143

Chapter 11: **Information Governance**
by Galina Datskovsky, Ph.D., CRM...................................157

Chapter 12: **Governance and Sustainability**
by Steve Boston 183

Appendix A: Corporate Governance Principles of CA, Inc............207

Appendix B: Compliance and
Risk Committee Charter of CA, Inc. 225

Index...231

About the Authors

Jacob Lamm is executive vice president of Strategy and Corporate Development at CA. In this role, he is responsible for coordinating the company's overall business strategy, as well as developing strategy for the selection, prioritization, and execution of acquisitions. In addition, Jacob leads CA's Business Incubation business units, which are charged with exploring opportunities to build businesses in new markets. He is also a member of CA's Executive Leadership Team, which defines and ensures execution of the Company's business and technical strategies.

Jacob has held various management positions since joining CA in 1998. Prior to assuming his current role he served as executive vice president of CA's Governance Group, a collection of business units focused on delivering solutions that help organizations effectively govern all areas of operations. Earlier, he was executive vice president and general manager of CA's Business Service Optimization business unit.

Jacob has more than 20 years of industry experience covering a wide range of technologies and business applications.

He joined CA with its acquisition of Professional Help Desk (PHD), where he was co-founder and served as executive vice president and chief technology officer. Under his leadership, PHD evolved into one of the strongest products on the market and gained industry recognition as having the most visionary service management solution.

Prior to founding PHD, Jacob served as a senior manager at Con Edison in New York, where he was responsible for integrating new technologies into the company's business systems, including wireless communications, data warehousing, imaging, and Internet solutions. A graduate of Brooklyn College, Jacob earned a bachelor's degree in computer information science.

Sumner Blount is the director of Product Marketing for the GRC business unit at CA. He is responsible for product positioning, and is a significant contributor to thought-leadership activities related to GRC. Prior to this role, he was the director of Solutions Marketing for the Security Management business unit.

Sumner joined CA from Netegrity, where he served as the senior product manager for SiteMinder for three years. Prior to Netegrity, he managed the large computer operating system development group at Digital Equipment and Prime Computer, and was director of software for Pathway Designs. He later was instrumental in the original conception and development of the DCE (Distributed Computing Environment) technology from the Open Software Foundation, and served as the DCE program manager within Digital. He has held a number of product management positions, including management of the Distributed Computing Product Management group at Digital.

His articles have appeared in several industry publications including Compliance Executive Journal, Business Management Journal and Mainframe Executive and he has spoken at a number of industry conferences.

Sumner received a Bachelor of Science degree in Math from the University of North Carolina, and a Masters degree in Computer Science from the University of Connecticut.

Steve Boston is vice president and chief sustainability officer at CA. He is responsible for CA's worldwide sustainability efforts. Steve works on various initiatives applying IT technology to foster solutions for environmental and social issues. He is currently focused on driving the development of energy management technologies.

Steve brings historical and big-picture perspectives to technical and operational issues and leverages business intelligence to expand CA's ability to positively impact our planet and communities.

During Steve's 20 year career in the IT industry, prior to joining CA, he held positions in strategy, development and management. Steve was a member of IBM's Software Group Strategy unit and led an effort to determine where Digital Media fit into IBM's overall strategy and helped to define the company's Itanium II positioning.

Steve has filed more than 25 patent applications in various emerging technology areas. He participates in CA's Technology Innovation Committee and is a member of CA's Council for Technical Excellence.

Steve serves as member of the U.S. Council for Competitiveness on the Energy, Security, Innovation and Sustainability committee. He is also a member of the World Economic Forum's Committee for Information and Communication Technology.

Steve attended Northeastern University where he majored in business.

Marc Camm is senior vice president and general manager of Governance, Risk and Compliance products at CA. He is responsible for establishing CA as a leader in the emerging GRC market.

Marc joined CA in 2003 through the acquisition of Adjoin and has since held a number of management positions. Prior to assuming his current role, he served as the vice president and general manager of CA's mobile device management business unit, which was focused on securing and managing Smartphone technology in the enterprise. Earlier, he was vice president and general manager of CA's Managed Vulnerability Service, which was the forerunner of CA's first Software as Service offering. Marc has been instrumental in conceiving, developing and expanding CA's new business opportunities.

Prior to joining CA, Marc was chief operating officer of Adjoin, responsible for marketing, sales, business development, and product management groups. A 20-year software industry veteran, Marc has held senior management positions at Microsoft, Symantec, Delrina and BindView in addition to working with several other technology startups.

Marc received a Bachelor of Commerce degree from the University of Manitoba in Canada.

Robert Cirabisi is CA's senior vice president and chief risk officer, responsible for overseeing the company's worldwide Enterprise Risk Management Function and Global Quality and Controls.

In his role as chief risk officer, Bob is responsible for examining the company's activities and establishing a framework to protect the company against significant risks, both internal and external, and to consider significant risks, trends and uncertainties arising with respect to the company's strategies, business operations, financial reporting, and legal and regulatory affairs. This role reports dually to CA's Chief Administrative Officer and to the Compliance and Risk Committee of the Board of Directors. Bob is also responsible for the prioritization and global rollout of CA's GRC Manager product across CA's various business functions.

Bob joined CA in 2000 and has held various positions including chief audit executive, corporate controller, acting chief financial officer, chief accounting officer, vice president of Investor Relations and U.S. controller.

Prior to joining CA, Bob had over 13 years of audit experience with Ernst & Young and Arthur Anderson, specializing in its energy and utility practice. Bob is a Certified Public Accountant and a graduate of Hofstra University in Hempstead NY.

 **Nancy E. Cooper**, executive vice president and chief financial officer, is responsible for all of CA's corporate and business unit financial functions worldwide, including the controller role, treasury, tax, investor relations, and risk management. Nancy joined CA in August of 2006.

Nancy has nearly 30 years of finance experience, most recently serving as chief financial officer for IMS Health, Incorporated, a leading provider of market intelligence to the pharmaceutical and healthcare industries. There, her responsibilities included finance and accounting, treasury, investor relations, human resources, and business development. She was instrumental in integrating IMS' financial systems and finance teams representing more than 100 countries and closing 30 acquisitions IMS made during her tenure.

Prior to joining IMS Health, Nancy was the chief financial officer of Reciprocal, Inc., a leading digital rights management and consulting firm whose clients included McGraw Hill, Sony, Time Warner, and Reuters. In addition, she served as chief financial officer of Pitney Bowes Credit Corporation, an international credit company. In 1998, Nancy served as a partner responsible for finance and administration at General Atlantic Partners, a private equity firm focused on software and services investments.

From 1976 to 1998, Nancy held various positions of increasing responsibility at IBM, including CFO of the Global Industries Division, assistant corporate controller, and controller and treasurer of IBM Credit Corporation. Prior to that, she served as director of Financial Management Systems, Pricing and Financial Planning at IBM, responsible for pricing strategy and financial planning management among many IBM divisions worldwide.

Nancy holds a Bachelor of Arts degree in Economics and Political Science from Bucknell University and an MBA from the Harvard Graduate School of Business Administration.

Dr. Galina Datskovsky, Ph.D., CRM, is senior vice president and general manager of the Information Governance business unit at CA, responsible for the CA Message Manager and CA Records Manager product lines. She is also recognized as a Distinguished Engineer at CA, and joined the company in 2006 with the acquisition of MDY Group International, where she served as founder and CEO.

Prior to founding MDY, Galina consulted for IBM and Bell Labs and taught at the Fordham University Graduate School of Business and the Graduate School of Arts and Sciences at Columbia University.

Galina received her Certified Records Manager (CRM) certification in 2004 and is recognized around the world as an expert in records management and associated technologies, including the convergence of records and document management, email and physical records management, and federated records management.

She has been widely published in academic journals and speaks frequently for industry organizations such as AIIM, Association of Legal Administrators, Gilbane Conferences, LawNet/ILTA and Cohasset Associates/MER. Galina also serves on the board of ARMA International, a not-for-profit Information Management education organization.

Galina earned her BA from Barnard College and doctoral and master's degrees in Computer Science from Columbia University.

Christopher Fox is a senior principal in CA's Governance Risk and Compliance Manager group. Part of his role is to focus on the evolution of GRC, provide CA thought leadership and to translate new developments into requirements for future versions of our software. Where knowledge has not been fully defined, Chris helps to refine and develop GRC intellectual property, including a risk library, and provide support to CA and the GRC market.

He became interested in GRC through work he performed at the Australian Securities Exchange and furthered his interest working as a director at PricewaterhouseCoopers in banking regulatory projects and in the management of large Sarbanes-Oxley projects. He has also provided IT input into COSO ERM, worked on the Monitor and Evaluate component in COBIT 4.1 and was one of the main authors of ISACA's IT Control Objectives for Sarbanes-Oxley and one of the authors for IT Control Objectives for Basel II. He was a member of the task force that developed OCEG's Red Book on GRC. He is currently working on an ISACA project addressing IT enabled monitoring of controls and a CA project mapping the Uniform Controls Library to FISMA requirements.

Kenneth V. Handal served as executive vice president, office of the chief executive officer, at CA. Until April 2009, he served as executive vice president, global risk & compliance and corporate secretary, with a responsibility for CA's corporate governance, risk and compliance programs, and the internal audit and global security functions. Ken joined the company in July 2004, as executive vice president, general counsel and corporate secretary.

Prior to joining CA, Ken was associate general counsel and served as compliance counsel for Altria, then the parent company of Kraft Foods and Philip Morris. Prior to joining Altria, Ken was a partner with the law firm of Arnold & Porter. Earlier, he was an Assistant United States Attorney for the Southern District of New York, Criminal Division. He also served as a law clerk to Judge Robert A. Ainsworth, Jr. of the U.S. Court of Appeals for the Fifth Circuit.

Ken currently serves on the advisory boards of the Hospital for Special Surgery and Corporate Counsel magazine. He has served on the boards of the National Center for Missing & Exploited Children, The Legal Aid Society, the Association of the Bar of the City of New York Fund, Inc., New York Lawyers for the Public Interest, the International League for Human Rights, the Brooklyn Academy of Music, and the Convent of the Sacred Heart. He also established the in-house Pro Bono Programs at

CA and Altria. Ken is a frequent lecturer at continuing legal education conferences.

Ken earned his law degree from The University of Chicago Law School, where he was managing editor of the Law Review, and his undergraduate degree from Georgetown University.

 **William E. McCracken** is the independent Chairman of the Board at CA. Bill joined CA's Board of Directors in 2005, became Chairman in 2007, and also served as chairman of its special litigation committee.

Prior to joining CA, Bill held numerous executive positions at IBM during his 36-year tenure, most recently as a member of the Chairman's Worldwide Management Council and general manager of IBM's printing division. He previously served as president of IBM's EMEA and Asia PC Company and as the general manager, marketing, sales and distribution for IBM PC Company.

Bill is active in the National Association of Corporate Directors, and is a commissioner of the 2009 Blue Ribbon Commission on Risk Governance. He is also a participant in the Chairmen's Forum of the Millstein Center for Corporate Governance and Performance at the Yale School of Management.

Bill is the president of Executive Consulting Group, LLC, and was a director of IKON Office Solutions. He is board chairman of Lutheran Social Ministries of New Jersey, a member of the New Jersey State Anti-Poverty Network, and a former president of the board of Plainfield Habitat for Humanity.

John Meyer is Vice President of Business Unit Strategy for CA. John has led strategy and product management for multiple business units since he joined CA in 2003. John's broad industry expertise both as an industry analyst and seasoned IT practitioner allows him to infuse CA's strategy with his big picture insights and real world customer driven experience across multiple IT domains.

During his 24 year career in the IT industry he has made significant contributions to the advancement of IT and business alignment. As a senior industry analyst at Forrester Research he provided insight and guidance to many Fortune 500 companies and was a recognized speaker within the IT industry often being quoted by the media. Prior to Forrester Research, John was Director of Enterprise Architecture (EA) for Fortune 50 Fannie Mae. He has also held technology leadership and management positions at other leading companies such as Oracle Corporation, Booz Allen and Hamilton, and Wellspring Resources.

John holds a Bachelor of Science degree in Computer Science from the University of Maryland.

Helge Scheil is CA senior vice president and area manager, responsible for the company's operations in Germany.

Prior to April 2009, Scheil was senior vice president and general manager of the Project and Portfolio Management business unit within the Governance group at CA, responsible for the CA Clarity PPM, New Product Development and Professional Services Automation product lines.

Scheil joined CA with its acquisition of Niku in July 2005. At Niku, he was responsible for all research and development activities and the creation of an innovative, extensible, scalable and fully globalized architecture for Clarity, the market-leading Project and Portfolio Management solution.

Scheil has more than 19 years of experience in enterprise business application development and consulting, a career that took him from Philips Medical System in Germany to Oracle's headquarters in California, where he held various development management positions.

Scheil holds a Bachelor of Science degree in Business and Computer Science from the University of Kiel, Germany.

Alan Srulowitz is vice president of Finance Strategy at CA. In this role, he is responsible for the design and implementation of a Finance Excellence Program to identify and prioritize changes to processes, systems and organizational structure that will improve the efficiency and effectiveness of the Finance organization.

Alan has held various management roles since joining CA in 2004. Prior to assuming his current role he led the Internal Control Function (ICF) to support management's compliance with the Sarbanes Oxley Act. In 2008, Alan was named a "Millstein Rising Star of Corporate Governance" by the Yale School of Management and was nominated for a Corporate Secretary Magazine Award in the "Rising Star" category.

Alan has extensive experience in auditing, finance and operational management. Before joining CA in 2004, Alan was the Controller of the Experience Music Project, an interactive music museum founded by Paul Allen. Earlier, he served in various management roles at Amazon.com supporting the build-out of their Global Logistics Division. Alan began his career as an auditor at KPMG.

Alan earned a Bachelor of Arts degree with high honors at Queens College and a Master of Business Administration degree from Columbia Business School. He is a Certified Public Accountant.

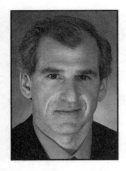

Rob Zanella is vice president of IT Compliance for CA and is responsible for all compliance activities within Information Technology. Rob joined CA in 2005 as director of Internal Audit to develop the company's first IT Audit practice. Upon establishing the practice, Rob next assumed responsibility for the IT Compliance function to advise on controls optimization opportunities and to manage CA's IT risk and controls profile.

Rob has 25 years of IT experience in operations, software development, project management, and auditing. Before joining CA, he was director of IT Audit for 5 years at SIAC, the technology arm of the NYSE. Prior to the NYSE, Rob was a senior manager at Deloitte & Touche for 7 years, implementing ERP solutions as part of their Enterprise Risk Services group for several large clients. In addition, he held various software development and project management positions within Savings Bank Trust Company and Union Savings Bank while developing and implementing lending software.

Rob has been a Certified Information Systems Auditor (CISA) as certified by ISACA (Information Systems Audit and Control Association) since 1995. He holds a Bachelor of Science in Computer Science from Hofstra University and a Master of Business Administration from Adelphi University.

Contributors

Christopher Boswell

Margaret Brooks

Terrence Clark

David Hurwitz

Lynne Iati

Lily Kang

Elizabeth Kelly

Tom Kendra

Yves Le Roux

Lynne Mahoney

Bill Manago, CRM

Michael Mattia

Thomas McHale

Jeffrey Meyer

Jose Mora

Kristen Perdue

Steve Romero

Michael Sanchez, Sirius Solutions

Peter Stapleton

Kurt Steinle

Robert Stubbs

Andrew Wittman

Acknowledgments

The authors gratefully acknowledge the help and support of a number of individuals who made up the project team.

Their CA colleagues: Lynne Mahoney, whose determination, resourcefulness and editing drove the book to completion; Sumner Blount, who both authored his own chapters and made invaluable contributions to many others; Connie Smallwood and Karen Sleeth, who worked tirelessly to establish the CA Press infrastructure; Andrew Wittman, whose critical thinking helped both launch and complete the project; Margaret Brooks for contributing her subject matter expertise to the reviewing effort; Lily Kang for her valuable work on "Governance of Risk and Compliance"; Michael Mattia for his widespread contributions to "IT Governance, Risk and Compliance"; Elizabeth Kelly for her substantial work on "Governance and Portfolio Management" and Steve Romero for reviewing same and contributing blog posting; Robert Stubbs for his extensive editing of "The Regulatory Environment"; Bill Manago, CRM, for lending his expertise to "Information Governance"; Jeffrey Meyer for his extensive work on "Governance and Sustainability". Terrence Clark for reviewing same and contributing his blog posting.

Their partners at Apress, Inc.: Jeffrey Pepper and James Markham (the editorial team); Tiffany Taylor for her editing work; Tom Welsh for fact checking; Frank McGuckin for directing the production of the book; Anna Ishchenko for her work on the cover; April Milne and Jerry Votta for the art; and especially James Keogh for all of his work on the book.

Introduction

Business and public sector leaders today face an unprecedented challenge of compliance and risk management.

A long-standing trend toward increased regulation became a flood with the economic crisis of 2008. Combined with the clamor for improved enterprise risk management and the growing complexity of multi-national compliance, these conditions present executives with a dramatically new and confusing array of questions and challenges.

Governance should offer solutions, but it is increasingly clear that yesterday's governance practices aren't up to the task. In both design and implementation, they are too disconnected and incomplete to fully address our complex compliance and risk management puzzle. Executives get only fragmented views of their true business performance, and inefficiencies drive up costs.

We at CA can look at this challenge with a unique perspective. As Computer Associates, our company directly experienced the consequences of inadequate governance, including an investigation in 2002 that resulted in an agreement with the government to improve accounting and other business processes. Those who know this history may wonder why CA is qualified to advise on governance at all. My answer is, who could better understand the issues and the consequences of inadequate governance than CA?

In our exhaustive efforts to successfully rebuild our company, we have worked with the leading thinkers in governance and ethics. Where some companies view governance as a "nice to have", seeking out and implementing best practices in the field was essential to CA's future. That imperative allowed us to devote a significant amount of energy and resources to the task, and attracted some of the best people in the field to CA. Our improvements enabled us to fulfill our obligation to the government, stabilized the company, and propelled us into a new era of growth with an unusually strong foundation of leading governance practices.

In this book, we have captured that expertise for the benefit of other organizations. Each chapter is authored by a CA executive with in-the-trenches responsibility for vital governance processes, and in some cases the development of governance solutions. Those solution experts have worked with thousands of clients, giving them unparalleled insight into the most practical and productive governance practices.

Our collaboration as a team, leveraging both CA and external experience, led us to formulate a new approach to governance that unifies compliance and risk management to increase the effectiveness, and decrease the cost, of both. The core of this unified approach is the centralization of policies across organizational silos. Polices include any requirement on the IT infrastructure, employee behavior, or business processes that enable an organization to reach its goals. Too often these policies are recorded, implemented and measured in organizational silos. But for really effective governance, we need to break down the walls between those silos and devise common approaches to managing policies, measuring performance against them, and ensuring compliance with them.

And, this management of policies must be executed with formality, rigor and transparency. That allows governance to become part of the fabric of an organization with defined, documented, communicated and repeatable processes. With this approach, we can develop and maintain policies that address the current governance need—and have enough flexibility to address evolving market conditions.

This unified governance approach also offers a broad view of risk across the enterprise. It standardizes risk management rather than isolating it to individual regulatory or operational silos. Organizations gain not only greater insight into risk within business units, but also can evaluate the interactions of risks across the enterprise and more easily identify emerging risks before they become critical to the entire organization.

And finally, risk management and compliance will be under control.

Jacob Lamm
Executive Vice President, CA, Inc.

The Rise of Governance

by Jacob Lamm

Rumblings deep in the world economy drew little attention in 2006. Interest rates rose modestly and housing prices stopped their steep ascent in the United States, signaling an economic swing that financial institutions normally handle in stride.

However, this time conditions were different. Proven techniques for dealing with economic swings couldn't handle the events that were to unfold at lightning speed. The United States housing bubble finally burst in 2008—creating the most serious financial crisis since the Great Depression.

The house of cards tumbled, taking with it several cornerstone financial institutions. Certain corporate leaders were stunned and wondered how such strong organizations with sophisticated technology at their fingertips failed to foresee and react to such a devastating exposure to risk. And many were surprised at how large the impact was. Banks and other financial companies, as well as their investors, were dramatically hit as the effect rippled throughout the world.

The reason was, in essence, tunnel vision. Leaders of some of the world's marquee corporations were blindsided because their internal corporate monitors were unable to piece together regulatory, operational, and risk-management indicators that pointed to irregularities and which collectively jeopardized the underpinnings of their businesses.

The subprime-mortgage crisis was the latest event to highlight shortcomings in corporate governance. Many past failures, including that of Enron, were often the result of poor corporate oversight. In some cases, out-and-out fraud was involved. However, fraud that goes undetected or unaddressed is, to some extent, a failure of corporate governance.

As these cases appear in the news, cries for stronger and more effective governance, often accompanied by more stringent governmental regulation, go out. In many cases, these governance "holes" are plugged or at least mitigated—until the next governance crisis. This creates a need for increased emphasis on improved governance, and the cycle continues.

What Does Governance Really Mean?

Like many terms in the public eye in recent months, *governance* is in the eye of the beholder, and definitions can vary from one author to another. But the essence of the definitions is generally the same. *Governance* is the leadership, organizational structures and processes that help ensure that an organization's functions sustain and extend its strategies and objectives. Put more simply, it is the culture, policies, procedures and controls that help ensure a company will meet its business goals.

Governance is "everybody's job." However, the key governance responsibilities are typically entrusted to the Board of Directors and the executive management of a corporation who are responsible for providing the oversight that is intended to help ensure that a company meets its goals.

When considering the broad topic of governance, an obvious question might be "Governance of *what?*" The answer is "Governance of everything that relates to the operation of the company." This includes a wide variety of areas, such as finance, marketing, product development, security, information technology (IT), human resources, compliance, risk, and others.

There are a few generally accepted terms for the different areas of governance. Let's review the most common ones:

Corporate governance focuses on the effectiveness of the corporation as a whole, including meeting defined risk and compliance goals, so as to meet the overall business objectives. This is the responsibility of executive management, the Board of Directors, and often the legal department.

Corporate governance is the application of formality, rigor, and transparency to a unified framework of corporate policy, to help ensure that an organization takes on only prudent risks in its quest to return stockholder value and succeed in the market. (See the section "A New, Unified Approach" later in this chapter for more on formality, rigor, and transparency.) Risks that affect the achievement of strategic goals must be understood, properly assessed, and managed effectively.

Operational governance focuses on the planning and execution of projects and resources associated with key business operations, such as IT and product development. The focus here is on ensuring that the operational processes of the company are effective and efficient, and that assets of all types are used effectively to help meet corporate goals.

Governance, risk, and compliance (GRC) focuses on the activities related to the governance of regulatory requirements, enterprise risk areas such as financial and IT risk, compliance controls, and information across the enterprise. GRC is not a specific function in an organization, but rather an integrated approach across multiple business functions related to the management of risk, controls, and compliance.

Historically, this management has often been handled by disparate groups with minimal interaction. More recently, there's been a trend toward a more unified view of these areas to help controls costs, eliminate redundancy, and improve the quality of the information that is used to make decisions related to risk and compliance.

GRC includes several different but related areas:

- *Enterprise risk management* focuses on predicting and managing events that might impact the achievement of business goals.

- *Financial GRC* relates to the quality, timeliness, and transparency of financial statements and transactions of the company.

- *IT GRC* relates to managing IT risk and ensuring that the IT infrastructure supports corporate compliance needs.

- Finally, *information governance* focuses on ensuring that the company's information assets are known, categorized, and available when needed.

Figure 1-1 illustrates the relationships of these areas to each other.

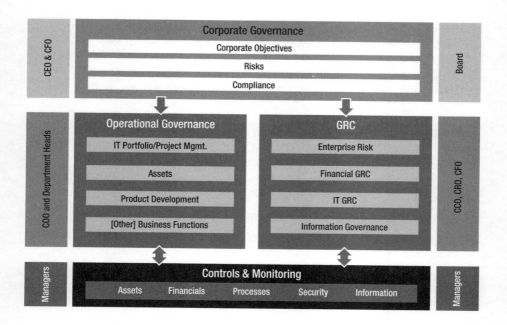

Figure 1-1. Areas of governance

A key element of all these different areas of governance is the design, implementation, continuous monitoring, and auditing of compliance controls to assess the organization's vital signs, enabling corporate leaders to oversee activities and intervene, if necessary, to put the organization back on course.

The Drivers for Governance

Governance is far from a new concept; corporations have long practiced it. But there *has* been a change in the level of attention given to governance. This increased emphasis has been driven by the needs of the corporation, the stockholders, and regulatory bodies. The following are some of the key business drivers for improved corporate governance.

The Rise of Risk

Recent economic events have shown clearly that the improper assessment and management of risk can have a catastrophic impact on a corporation. The precise causes of the recent economic crisis are open to debate, but it's clear that ineffective or nonexistent risk management was a significant contributing factor.

In its policy paper "Climbing Out of the Credit Crunch",[1] the Association of Chartered Certified Accountants, the international accountancy body, pointed to the failure of corporate governance at some financial institutions as the underlying cause of this catastrophe. This failure led to excessive risk-taking and insufficient risk management.

Where did this emphasis on risk come from? From a painful history.

On July 30, 2002, the Sarbanes-Oxley Act (SOX), which implemented some of the most far-reaching reforms of public companies since Franklin D. Roosevelt's New Deal, was signed into law. SOX sought to increase transparency, improve the accuracy of financial statements, and reduce potential conflicts of interest.

Prior to SOX, outside auditors could enter into lucrative consulting contracts with clients they audited. Securities analysts could issue "buy" recommendations for corporations who paid substantial bank service fees to the investment banking side of the house. The extensive use of stock options to compensate executives at certain corporations created pressure

---

[1] Association of Chartered Certified Accountants, "Climbing Out of the Credit Crunch," September 2008, http://www.accaglobal.com/allnews/national/australia/3150218 (accessed 1 December 2009).

to "make the numbers," even if that meant taking greater risk. This was sometimes coupled with a lack of transparency because stock options were not treated or reported as compensation expenses.

Prior to SOX, the audit committees of some public corporations failed to establish adequate oversight for financial reporting. There was limited oversight within some corporations for monitoring executive decisions, and little information or authority to question corporate decision-making.

The new SOX corporate governance environment set rules for governance and established penalties for executives whose failure to govern effectively led to a violation of SOX. Management and external auditors were required to perform top-down risk assessments to identify and prevent fraud and safeguard assets. Financial risks had to be mitigated by implementing internal controls over financial reporting. These internal controls had to be created, documented, and tested, and their accuracy and effectiveness had to be verified by external auditors.

SOX was intended to increase transparency, and therefore help ensure that a company's financial reporting is accurate. One of its goals was to reduce the probability of corporate fraud on the level of Enron, Global Crossing, and several others.

Why, then, didn't the requirements of SOX preclude the occurrence of the recent financial crisis? It is possible for a company to comply with SOX and still make very bad business decisions or investments? In the recent crisis, many companies made bad investments that, in hindsight, may have been too risky. Some companies may even have been purposely misled. But this was a failure of business prudence and risk management, not of financial transparency.

It's a Regulatory Jungle Out There

Recently, a host of regulations and industry best practices have been introduced that encourage executives to exercise greater oversight over the operation of their corporation. Each regulation and best practice imposes standards that set the bar for internal corporate performance. Failure to comply with regulations could jeopardize revenue flow and business relationships, and expose the corporation to legal actions and government sanctions.

Let's look at some of the most well-known and commonly applied regulations:

- *The Sarbanes-Oxley Act (SOX)*, as discussed previously, is intended to help ensure the accuracy and transparency of corporate financial statements. It requires management of public companies to include, as part of their annual report, a report on internal controls over financial reporting. And it has teeth—shareholders can sue corporate directors for breach of their heightened duties. In some extreme cases, corporate executives have been convicted of felonies for violating this law.

- SOX has meant significant pain and cost for many companies due to the sweeping changes in organizational practices that it has engendered. And, as additional regulations are introduced, costs may further increase. As a result, there is a strong movement toward a more unified compliance approach in order to avoid the one-off costs of complying with regulations individually.

- The *Payment Card Industry Data Security Standard (PCI DSS)* is a comprehensive framework that provides security, data integrity, and privacy for processing electronic credit card payments. Businesses, from small mom-and-pop operations to national retailers, must adhere to these standards or face stiff fines. But because PCI DSS is essentially an industry standard (promulgated by the credit card-issuing companies), the framework doesn't carry the force of law. If a company doesn't comply, that company won't be able to process credit card transactions (which may put the company out of business), but noncompliance on its own wouldn't result in criminal sanctions.

- The *Health Insurance Portability and Accountability Act (HIPAA)* ensures that an individual's health information is protected while still providing the patient's healthcare providers with information to care for the patient. HIPAA defines the use of protected health information and establishes the patient's rights to protect that information.

- Although this regulation impacts a range of companies—any company that stores or processes confidential health information—adherence (and therefore enforcement and penalties) has been somewhat spotty. However, the American Recovery and Reinvestment Act of 2009 (also known as the 2009 Stimulus Bill) passed by Congress greatly expanded the number of companies covered by the HIPAA requirements, as well as increased the penalties for noncompliance. As a result, enforcement of HIPAA is likely to be increased.

- The *Gramm-Leach-Bliley Act (GLBA)* governs the collection and disclosure of customers' personal financial information by both financial and nonfinancial firms. It requires corporations to design, implement, and maintain safeguards to protect that financial information.

The above provides a limited view of just a handful of the major regulations that impact companies today. Although these mandates have a decidedly United States focus, similar mandates throughout the world demand compliance from any company doing business in a given country. Such mandates illustrate the recent increase in regulatory demands by governmental agencies, as well as by industry groups.

The Cost of Compliance

Another key business driver for effective governance is cost. Many corporations have found that SOX compliance is significantly more painful and costly than they expected, in part due to the fact that they didn't have the controls in place that were required for SOX compliance. It has been estimated that SOX compliance could cost $1 million for every $1 billion of corporate revenue[2]. And for small corporations, where compliance cost can be a crippling factor, that ratio is even worse. Exacerbating this problem is the fact that the law itself does not prescribe specifically what is required in order to be in compliance. Instead, the law states that companies must have effective controls sufficient to ensure the accuracy of financial statements.

---

[2] Steve Ranger, "IT the key to cutting SOX costs," ZDNet Asia, 16 November 2005. http://www.zdnetasia.com/news/business/0,39044229,39291246,00.htm (accessed 1 December 2009).

As a result, many companies look to industry best practices, such as those developed by the Committee of Sponsoring Organizations (COSO) of the Treadway Commission, which established frameworks to guide management, or the International Organization for Standardization (ISO),which provided specific descriptions of what is needed in order to achieve compliance. Whatever the source, the requirements can cause major changes to companies' internal corporate practices, resulting in high costs and extreme frustration.

There is often a high opportunity cost for all this effort. Compliance costs—auditors, consultants, lawyers, computer applications—are a significant drain on manpower and revenue, especially when that effort is often duplicated for each set of regulations. Some executives have expressed the view that while the intent of regulations benefits shareholders, the expense many times outweighs this benefit.

Globalization and Complexity

Corporate governance of all kinds is particularly challenging in today's environment. Increased globalization has introduced complexity across all industries.

For example, each country has a multitude of government agencies and business associations issuing mandatory or strongly recommended regulations for conducting business within its borders. Failure to comply exposes a corporation to economic sanctions that may jeopardize its ability to compete in the local market. This problem would be severe enough if it were only an issue of multiple regulations across countries. But when these regulations actually conflict with each other, as they sometimes do, the complexity can become daunting.

Some regulations are relatively uniform among countries, such as those in the 27-member European Union (EU), which helps to reduce the complexity of becoming compliant. However, outside the EU, many regulations are different and at times competing, resulting in a monumental challenge for corporate compliance officers. For example, the U.S.-based SOX regulation requires a company to institute some form of whistleblower process to guarantee that employees who want to report corporate fraud or illegal activity are free from retaliation by management. The motivation for this requirement is clear and logical. However, France, for instance, has laws that preclude this type of mechanism, under the principle that it could be used to violate an individual's privacy.[3] As a result, multinational companies may have significant challenges when faced with meeting the whistleblower requirements of SOX or developing a consistent set of policies for the handling and communication of consumers' confidential information.

The Challenge of Information Silos

As large companies struggled with their compliance challenges, they have often attempted to solve them on a regulation-by-regulation basis. This has resulted in *information silos*—pockets of information spread around an organization that contain similar (or in some cases identical) data relating to compliance activities. Of course, when the same information is stored in multiple places, the likelihood of inconsistency is high. This is a pernicious problem because the people who rely on this information may not be aware of the existence of the silos.

A simple (and common) example is that of a SOX program team that conducts a test of SOX controls, some of which are failing to operate effectively. The SOX team can attempt to initiate a project to remediate its controls. But suppose these controls also are used for PCI compliance, and the PCI program team is not aware of these control failures. The result is higher risk for PCI noncompliance, but that increased risk may not be visible to upper management.

Information silos also result in a significant amount of duplicated work, with some controls getting tested redundantly simply because information about previous tests is scattered around the organization in multiple spreadsheets. Additionally, silos make it very hard to identify the total costs of compliance, since cost information tends to be dispersed and, more importantly, not tracked on a formal basis across the organization. The result is that some companies spend much more on compliance than is necessary or than they are aware of.

---

[3] Commission nationale de l'informatique des libertes (CNIL), http://www.cnil.fr (accessed 1 December 2009).

As with almost any problem that stems from duplicated information, the situation only gets worse over time. And as this happens, getting access to timely and correct governance information can become a big challenge.

The SOX project management office, the compliance office, the privacy office, internal auditors, legal counsel, and other silos responsible for regulatory and best-practice compliance conduct regular reviews. Each asks executives for information to assist in risk assessment and compliance appraisal, and those requests are often uncoordinated. Some large organizations have implemented one or more automated compliance systems but have not integrated those systems enterprise-wide.

Executives and staff take time away from the business to assemble and review information that may already exist in a different silo. Even in corporations with well-developed systems, data coming from disparate departments may be missing required information, adding to the effort required by the corporation to manage compliance. Executives must be prepared to present evidence of their company's compliance. This can be a daunting task, since executives are experts in running the business, but not generally experts in compliance.

Ensuring compliance is important, however; noncompliance has the potential to impact operations. To ensure compliance, an executive might be directed to change the way business is conducted, including implementing new procedures, introducing new IT applications and equipment, and retraining staff, all while continuing to fulfill the organization's primary charter to increase value to customers and return a profit to stockholders.

A New, Unified Approach,

The existence of risk and compliance silos has created a number of problems, as described earlier. As the influx of regulations continues, the complexity of multinational compliance increases, and the demands for effective enterprise risk management grow, executives are looking for new governance practices. They need to unify their approaches to compliance challenges and risk management efforts to increase the effectiveness and decrease the cost of both areas.

At the heart of unified risk management and compliance is *corporate policy*. Policies include any requirements on the IT infrastructure, employee behavior, or business processes that help a company meet its overall business goals. Corporate leaders need to link together the silos by devising a common way to manage policy, measure performance against policy, and help ensure compliance with policies and objectives—while maintaining the *formality*, *rigor*, and *transparency* of efficient governance.

Formality provides a defined, documented, communicated, repeatable process for developing and maintaining policies to meet the current and changing market and the regulatory environment. *Rigor* requires a solid rationale for corporate policy, based on best practices, guidelines, and regulations. *Transparency* is a crucial ingredient of effective and efficient governance in that it:

- Clarifies how risk is managed so corporate leaders are aware of corporate exposure and can therefore help ensure that contingency plans are available.

- Allows a view into the condition of the organization beyond a few top managers, thereby enabling a system of checks and balances.

- Helps ensure that policies are managed properly and communicated to the organization.

- Identifies how corporate leaders measure success so the organization and outside interests can use these measurements to determine adherence to corporate policies.

A unified governance approach provides corporate leaders with a broad view of corporate policies, expected outcomes, and associated risks across the entire organization. It leads to a unified view of risk across the enterprise that helps organizations standardize risk management, manage existing risks more effectively, and recognize emerging risks before they affect the business.

Conclusion

Earlier in this decade, several high-profile corporate fraud cases led to increased regulatory mandates. Systemic failures that led to recent economic turmoil are triggering new regulations and new operational and risk management indicators that are intended to strengthen a corporation's financial underpinnings. As the complexity of managing risk and compliance increases, organizations need to evolve their approaches to these areas.

What worked in the past is unlikely to work in this new and more complex environment. To succeed, organizations must break down silos to achieve a unified approach to governance, risk, and compliance.

In the following chapters, we'll explore governance throughout various aspects of the organization: from its effect on departments to its effect on the Board of Directors; from how it shapes the management of information, to how it shapes the management of risk; from its relationship with IT, to its relationship with sustainability.

Let's take a closer look at governance across the enterprise.

Governance Today

by Jacob Lamm

The recent emergence of governance, risk, and compliance (GRC) initiatives in organizations throughout the world has generated a lot of market buzz and interest among analysts and executives alike. In such an environment, there may be some confusion about the terms *governance*, *risk*, and *compliance*, and how they differ from each other. Many organizations manage compliance on a regulation-by-regulation basis, or as separate projects across departments. They fail to take advantage of synergies that exist across these compliance projects. Similarly, risk is often managed as a totally separate initiative, with relatively little connection or unification with the corporate compliance program. And finally, governance efforts are often ill-defined and not formalized, and bear little relationship to the corporate risk management or compliance programs.

These disjointed approaches to risk and compliance are problematic for a number of reasons. Briefly, these approaches create redundant information and activity, incur high costs, and make it difficult for executive management to get the right information that will enable them to make effective, risk-based decisions.

Let's look at some definitions of the GRC components and see how they relate to each other.

Risk is a measure of the impact of uncertainty on the achievement of strategic business goals. *Risk management* is a process used by an organization to determine how much risk it is willing to take, to identify risks to its business, and to develop a risk mitigation plan based on its business goals. Internal controls are used to monitor and mitigate negative risk across the entire organization. But risk management also includes permitting activities through which the organization may undertake prudent risk in order to take advantage of business opportunities. The goal of risk management is to reduce loss (due to negative risk) and to create value for the company (through prudent risk-taking).

Compliance is the act of adhering to, and demonstrating adherence to, external laws and regulations, as well as internal corporate policies, procedures, and controls.

Risk management and compliance are two of the most important activities that companies engage in. Both of these areas represent a set of processes within the company and generally have well-defined responsibilities, stakeholders (both internal and external), and metrics.

Governance is different. It is not a single set of processes, nor is it as measurable as risk and compliance. Governance is the culture, policies, procedures, and controls that create the environment and structure by which companies are managed. Governance, for example, includes the *oversight* of the company's risk management and compliance programs to help ensure that they meet strategic, business, legal, and ethical requirements as interpreted by the Board of Directors and executive management. Governance is a broader concept than risk management or compliance. It includes all aspects of corporate oversight, not just a single, specific area such as risk or compliance.

Now that we've defined governance, risk, and compliance, we need to define the acronym *GRC*, which is in popular use today. As with the other terms we discussed, the definition of GRC is subject to varied interpretations. Any formalized oversight activities on the part of executive management constitutes governance. But the term *GRC* specifically refers to the governance of risk and compliance, and all of the activities that relate to it.

The Goals of Governance

Governance activities and initiatives are designed and executed with two primary goals in mind:

1. **Create value for the corporation**. Building value is possibly the most important goal of a corporation. This is what provides returns to shareholders, creates opportunities for employees, and helps sustain corporate life during challenging economic times.

   Risk management has a large role to play in creating value, since taking prudent risks for financial gain is the key to sustaining and building corporate value. These risks include entering new markets, expanding geographically, changing the marketing strategy of the company, and even deciding to continue with a business that is not yet profitable. These are all risks related to growing a business.

   In addition, effective management of negative risk preserves value because it reduces or eliminates the probability of events that can have a dramatic negative impact on value. Investors don't like surprises— especially large, negative ones. A company that manages risks well tends to be valued more highly (all other things being equal) than a company that does not. Analysts and investors begin to trust the company's earnings projections and with that, confidence that the business is being run effectively.

2. **Create transparency.** Transparency implies that management can effectively determine how the company is operating, where the risks are, and whether corporate policies and mandates are being followed throughout the organization. *Transparency* is essentially management's window into the internal workings of the company. The clearer the window, the better the ability to manage the organization effectively. Without this visibility, executives may be flying blind and unable to determine the current state of the organization.

   The current drive for transparency arose from the corporate scandals several years ago of Enron, Global Crossing, and others. These events were, for the most part, the driving force behind the enactment of the

Sarbanes-Oxley Act (SOX). The goal of SOX was to require that public corporations establish adequate controls to help ensure transparency and the accuracy of financial statements. Transparency is an essential element of good governance not only because it is mandated by law, but because it enables executive management to understand the current state of the organization so that corrective action can be taken if necessary.

Counterexamples often provide excellent illustrations of key concepts. In 1995, Barings Bank collapsed under the weight of huge trading losses by a single rogue trader, Nick Leeson.[1] There were many failings in this sad situation, but one of the biggest was that Leeson was allowed to make trades with essentially no supervision by his management. Because there were no checks and balances (separation of duties), management did not notice his wild trading. There was a lack of transparency into his dealings, and therefore management did not realize the risk to which they were exposed. When the scheme was finally discovered, it was too late to save the institution.[2]

Note: There were many other problems at work here, including the fact that there *was* information available that should have raised red flags. For example, Mr. Leeson received awards for his trading volume, yet his management did not raise concerns when his own trading volume was a substantial portion of the total volume on the Singapore exchange. There was poor governance on many levels.)[3]

---

[1] Nick Leeson, "Rogue Trader," June 1997, http://www.nickleeson.com (accessed 1 December 2009).

[2] http://www.nickleeson.com

[3] http://www.nickleeson.com

You now know that the primary goals of governance activities are to create value and to create transparency. But how does this translate to day-to-day activities? What tasks actually comprise the governance of a corporation? Before we can answer these questions, we must note that governance includes three major areas:

1. **Setting corporate policies**: Define and communicate the rules and procedures with which all stakeholders must comply.

2. **Setting authority and responsibility levels**: Define and communicate the key roles for individuals involved in corporate oversight, and the specific responsibilities of each person.

3. **Ensuring accountability and oversight**: Define processes and feedback mechanisms so that progress toward governance goals can be measured and communicated.

These tasks are primarily the responsibility of executive management, who passes down the output of these tasks to lower levels of management for more granular implementation or enforcement. But simply passing them down is not sufficient to ensure effective governance. Communication mechanisms and monitoring practices need to be established to make sure overall accountability is in place and working effectively.

Governance Stakeholders

Although governance is primarily the responsibility of corporate management, its reach extends to all corners of a corporation. Good governance has to permeate the entire infrastructure of a company and its operations, at all levels. Although many companies believe they have good governance, their actions may miss the mark. They may focus solely on training to instill appropriate behavior in their employees. Companies that do this may be able to "check the box" for governance, but they are missing the point. Everyone in the organization should *understand* what governance means for their company and how governance is deployed and executed within the company. All employees should be familiar with how their own responsibilities relate to governance, as well as how those responsibilities impact the governance posture of their organization.

Figure 2-1 illustrates the levels of corporate management and the flow of information and responsibilities related to governance. Let's look at each level to understand in more detail a typical governance structure.

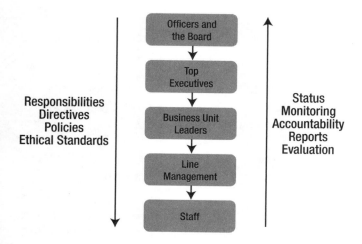

Figure 2-1. Governance stakeholders

The Board of Directors and the officers provide the top-level oversight of the entire enterprise. There is no area of governance that they don't ultimately own. They must define the core business goals and strategy of the corporation, as well as create and communicate the ethical standards under which they want the company to operate. These very broad strategies and standards get passed down to the rest of the organization and, at each level, they become more specific and prescriptive. Top executives communicate them (and possibly customize them for each business unit) down to the business unit executives, who then pass them down to the line managers. In many cases, of course, policies (particularly those related to ethical standards) get communicated directly from a top executive (such as the CEO), or a central group (such as HR or finance) to the employees as a whole. This tends to help ensure consistency of communication and serves to reinforce their importance as corporate mandates that everyone must follow.

Many people see governance as synonymous with management. This is unfortunate, because if your company is *governed* in the same way it is *managed*, it's likely that it is not being governed very effectively. Management tends to be hierarchical, and tends to have a one-directional communication flow. There is, of course, communication upward, but it is often limited.

Governance typically involves significant amounts of communication across many levels of the organization. Good governance is, in essence, a mechanism whereby people at all levels of the organization are aware of their responsibilities in terms of governance, and they communicate the status of their governance activities to other levels. This does not mean that an office worker in a cubicle will pick up the phone and call the CEO to update her on his current governance activities. It does mean, though, that the CEO can easily obtain information about the status of governance activities within that office worker's unit or department. In essence, governance information of all kinds flows in a circle, from executive management to line staff, and back again through the various levels of the organization.

This is often called *round-trip management* to emphasize the cyclical nature of it, and the fact that information flow is continuous and hits all levels of the organization. Without this level of continuous information flow, it's as if a directive is issued into a "black hole" without any ability to determine the level of compliance with that directive. A continuous, timely flow of information across levels of the organization is essential to achieve round-trip management, and is a key element of good corporate governance.

Governance in the Real World

In this chapter, you have seen how governance *should* work. We've identified the key goals of governance and looked at some of the activities that go into making a robust governance strategy.

So, how well does governance work in the real world? Judging by the circumstances of the 2008–2009 financial crisis . . . often not too well! Many analysts and pundits have published their views on how we got into this unpleasant situation, and I'm sure there will be many more to come. As of this writing, we don't know how long it will take for the economy to recover fully from this mess, and we certainly don't know yet what form of regulation will be introduced to attempt to avoid situations like this going forward. But it is a safe bet that there will be some sort of regulatory activity, possibly quite stringent, to try to reduce the probability of this kind of economic pain in the future.

Let's look at this situation from the point of view of governance and risk management, since these areas are at the core of this systemic failure. Putting on our governance glasses, we can see several causes of the crisis:

1. **"Best practices" were not used in the lending process**. In the past, there have been common best practices in lending that, for the most part, financial institutions have followed. These practices were based on the notion that you don't lend money to people who are not likely to pay the money back in a timely way. The reason that these practices were widely used was obvious—the people who lent the money were the ones who owned the risk, and they wanted to be paid back.

   Recently, as home prices skyrocketed, there was continued pressure to lend money for mortgages, gradually resulting in increasingly risky loans. These included such vehicles as adjustable-rate mortgages (ARMs), option ARMs, interest-only loans, and the infamous "liar loans." The latter were essentially loans made with little or no validation of the borrower's income, financial profile, or ability to pay back. Gradually, more and more people got mortgages but had less and less ability to pay them back. When housing prices declined precipitously, the house of cards became visible, and the collapse of the cards was painful.

2. **Loans became securitized, and their issuers overleveraged**. These shaky loans were packaged into very complex (and generally incomprehensible) financial instruments that were then sold to investors. The purchasers thought they were making solid investments (after all, few people default on their mortgages . . . right?). To make matters worse, quite often the loans were rated highly by the bond rating agencies because they were being offered by seemingly reputable institutions. Unfortunately, too few investors looked at the underlying mortgages to see if they had a reasonable chance of repayment. Also, as issuers sold these instruments, they took the proceeds and did more and more lending to even less-qualified borrowers. The amount of

leverage became excessive as risk piled upon risk.

3. **Risk became aggregated at central points**. As these risks increased, they aggregated at Fannie Mae, Freddie Mac, and mortgage insurance companies. The risks became oppressive, and financial instruments such as collateralized debt obligations (CDOs) only compounded the problem and put huge institutions at great risk.

Now you understand a bit about *how* the crisis happened. But it's also useful to look at *why* it happened. What failed? Was it a total lack of financial risk management? Was it greed? Was it lack of regulation? Was it all of these?

The cause of this crisis probably did include elements from all of these areas. There was unquestionably greed, but it's unlikely that we can legislate away human greed. Lack of appropriate regulation was probably also a causal factor, and we will soon see what regulatory remedies are in store for us. But in terms of risk management, several key failures deserve mention:

1. **Failure to embrace appropriate risk management behaviors**: Risk management needs to be an essential component in all key business processes, and every person who participates in those processes needs to be aware of the impact of their actions on risk and provide timely information that improves the management of risk related to that business process. In the current crisis, prudent risk management clearly was not integrated into the financial investment processes that determined the behavior of individual managers or traders.

2. **Failure to create and reward risk management competencies**: The individuals who were on the front lines taking financial risks were incented to maximize short-term profits, not to make prudent business decisions that would provide the best level of risk-return for the enterprise.

3. **Failure to use risk management to influence decision-making (for both risk-taking and risk-avoidance decisions)**: Even if the people on the front lines are diligent about their risk management responsibilities (and that is often not the case), unless this information related to risk is used proactively to inform and impact top management decision-making, its value is negated. Upper management either was not aware of the level of risk that their organization was taking on, or their incentives were skewed to the extent that they overlooked excessive short-term risk.

Conclusion

We have looked at the key goals of good governance, and some of the activities that this entails. We have also surveyed the types of roles that are typically involved in governance, and have seen how information and responsibility might flow among those groups. Finally, we have used the recent financial crisis to examine how governance and risk management can go *wrong*.

In the next chapter, we will look under the covers of governance to understand how it might be implemented within a corporation. In particular, we will look at the policy life cycle as a model for implementing the governance goals established by executive management and the Board of Directors.

Policy Management

by Sumner Blount

We have looked at some of the key goals of corporate governance, and some of the associated activities. We've also seen how governance extends into the organization, and some of the key organizational attributes that help support good governance. Let's turn now to the specific activities that are used to define and enforce good governance across the organization.

Governance is an ongoing process composed of the following general responsibilities:

1. Identifying business requirements.

2. Creating policies to meet these requirements.

3. Establishing controls to help ensure compliance with these policies.

4. Monitoring and remediating compliance controls.

Each of these steps is iterative, and the whole process uses feedback mechanisms to continually improve the overall effectiveness and efficiency of the corporation. Let's consider each of these areas and identify the key activities and responsibilities of each one.

Identifying Business Requirements

First, any company has a set of *business objectives* that they have established to help ensure the viability and growth of the enterprise. These are determined by executive management with oversight from the Board of Directors and then communicated downward into the organization. These objectives reflect the corporation's overall mission statement and are used to guide or direct employee behavior and decisions toward meeting the objectives. The mission statement is related to or contained within the charter or articles of incorporation issued by the state government for the founding stockholders.

Second, corporations must meet the *regulatory requirements* mandated by the government or by their industry. In some cases, compliance with regulations is mandated by law, for example, the Sarbanes-Oxley Act. In some cases, market forces serve to encourage compliance, for example, the Payment Card Industry Data Security Standard (PCI DSS). But in many cases, the distinction between law and market forces is arbitrary and not relevant to the compliance decisions made by upper management.

The third area of requirements addresses *enterprise risk*. Risk management is a very extensive topic that will be treated in more detail later in this book. But a quick summary is that enterprise risks need to be identified, categorized, and prioritized. These include risks across all areas, the major ones being financial risks, operational risks, IT risks, market risks, and external risks. As risks are identified and assessed, policies can be created to attempt to control the negative aspects of those risks, or to prudently manage any risks related to new business opportunities.

Creating Policies

To meet these requirements, companies create and enforce policies. A *policy* is a statement that embodies the goals and behavior that the company wants to instill in its employees and business partners. Policies are not immutable. They can change as new regulatory requirements arrive, as the business goals of the company change, or as the corporate risk-tolerance level changes.

In theory, all policies should be followed (or an exception should be approved under the policy provisions for exceptions), and there should be some sort of remedial action prescribed for noncompliance with a given policy. In reality, though, all policies are not created alike. The policy that prohibits employees from bribing governmental officials is likely to get much more emphasis and enforcement (hopefully!) than a policy relating to a much more mundane area, or one that is less critical to the successful operation of the business.

In general, regulatory requirements turn directly into company policies. If, for example, a company decides that it needs to comply with a given governmental or industry regulation, a set of corporate policies is created to define what level of compliance is required (even if the policy is simply "We will comply with this requirement").

Figure 3-1 illustrates the policy life cycle, from origination through ongoing revision.

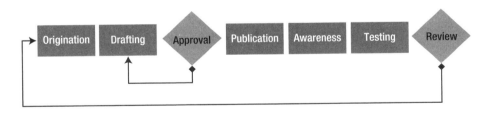

Figure 3-1. The policy life cycle

Management of corporate policies is an important element of governance. It needs to be much more than simply creating a document, sending it out to all employees, and then filing it away in a cabinet. Policy management includes a series of key steps, with feedback loops, intended to help ensure that policies are well communicated, fully understood by the target audience, and enforced.

Policies originate from various sources, as shown in Figure 3-1. Once the need for a policy has been identified, there are a number of steps to take to create, review, and communicate the policy. The following is a description of the process:

1. Clearly identify the risk to the organization, or the business objective that the policy is intended to address. A determination of the priority of this policy is helpful, because it will help you decide how best to communicate the policy and monitor compliance.

2. Review existing policies. Determine if interpretation of an existing policy might already address the risk, or if modification of an existing policy may suffice.

3. Draft a new policy (if necessary). On the surface, writing a policy seems fairly straightforward. However, the challenge is to find the right words to not only convey management's intent, but also to prevent that intent from being misinterpreted. Misinterpretation can lead to unintentional consequences. As a result, a complete policy review cycle that includes a variety of constituencies is essential. A policy that is determined to be defective after it has been widely communicated can be worse than having no policy at all.

4. Review the policy. Your major goals should be to ensure that the policy mitigates the risk, to ensure proper interpretation of the policy, and to identify unintentional consequences of the policy. Make sure the key constituencies are part of the review process. Update the policy as appropriate, based on feedback.

5. Approve the policy. There needs to be a clearly defined and preferably automated approval process (using a workflow).

When a policy is approved, there should be a formal process defined for management of the policy document. This can include a central repository, document versioning, edit histories, and other basic capabilities. Once a policy is published, awareness campaigns generally help ensure that all target users are aware of what the policy requires them to do or not to do. Finally, policy testing can be used where appropriate to help ensure that users actually understand the policy and how it relates to them. This is a measure both of the clarity of the policy itself and of the communication mechanism chosen to distribute it. Finally, there should be a periodic review cycle based on the calendar, or initiated when events dictate that the policy should be reviewed and updated. Policies that don't reflect current behavior norms or business realities can be worse than having no policies at all.

Figure 3-2 highlights the key steps of policy management.

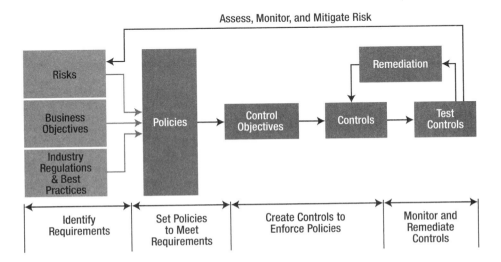

Figure 3-2. Key steps of policy management

Establishing Controls

In order to enforce its policies, an enterprise must translate them into a series of *control objectives*. These are statements of results that need to be achieved in order to enforce the policies. Control objectives are often reasonably non-specific, in that they describe the ultimate goal but do not define the actual mechanisms or processes (controls) that are required to achieve this objective. For example, a control objective might be "Only valid users will have accounts on all systems."

The control objectives will, in turn, be implemented by a set of *controls* to help ensure that the objectives are met. Controls are simply technologies, procedures, or a combination of the two that are intended to help ensure the correct operation of internal business processes.

Controls can generally be categorized as one of the following:

- *Preventative*: A preventative control stops a risk from occurring. For example, requiring an employee to enter a unique ID and password is a control that prevents unauthorized access to a computer application.

- *Detective*: A detective control identifies a problem when it occurs and communicates it to management. For example, a control might determine that the wrong password was entered three times and either lock the user out or notify the administrator, or both.

- *Corrective*: A corrective control attempts to rectify a problem once the problem is detected. For example, a control might search for accounts that were associated with terminated employees, and automatically remove those accounts.

Since controls are at the heart of both risk management and compliance, let's look at some simple examples of how they are implemented.

A common compliance requirement relates to segregation of duties (SOD). An SOD violation occurs any time one person or role has a privilege that introduces the possibility of a policy violation (such as fraud). Suppose an accounts payable clerk has the ability to enter new vendor records into the corporate database. Later, this person is promoted to be the accounts payable supervisor, who now has privileges to approve payments to vendors. Unless this person *loses* their original privileges to enter new vendor records, they could enter a fake vendor record and approve a payment to that vendor (who just happens to be this person's brother). A number of controls could be implemented to prevent this type of situation. They might include the following:

> When a person is promoted or changes roles, all their previous access privileges are immediately revoked, unless those privileges are required in the new role.

- A periodic program is run that captures each record of a vendor payment, and compares the Initiator field and the Approver field to check that the same person did not perform both operations.

Another common example of compliance controls occurs in the case of *orphan accounts*. These are system accounts that are live but do not have an owner. In some cases, the original owner has left the company but the account was never disabled. In other cases, an employee has changed roles but the account used in their previous role was never disabled. Both cases represent a security risk and therefore a compliance problem. As in the previous example, a number of controls can be instituted to combat the problem:

- When a person is promoted or changes roles, all their previous system accounts are disabled, unless those accounts are required in the new role.

- Whenever a person is terminated from the company (especially involuntarily), all their accounts are terminated within a timely manner.

- A program is run monthly that searches for all live accounts and compares the owner to the official list of employees to make sure the owner is still an employee.

Controls can be manual, automated, or a combination of the two. Any time a paper form or a signature is involved, the control is at least partly manual. In general, automation of controls is desirable for three reasons. First, it helps ensure consistency and reduces the risk of human error. Second, automated controls tend to be more auditable than manual controls because there is more likely to be "proof of compliance" available through event logs, audit trails, or the like. And finally, automated controls become much more scalable as the number of controls or users increases over time. For example, if the removal of accounts for a departed employee requires multiple administrators to physically go to multiple systems and manually remove those accounts, it would be time-consuming and error-prone, especially during times of high turnover. For a company with 50 employees, this might be tolerable. For a company with 10,000 employees, it could be a huge problem. An automated deprovisioning system might require a few keystrokes by the system administrator and be a much simpler, less time-consuming, more secure, and less error-prone solution.

Monitoring and Remediating Compliance Controls

Controls must be created, monitored, and reported to upper management to help ensure effective oversight. They must also be tested to help ensure compliance with policy, either on a scheduled or periodic basis. Controls are generally tested by a specific testing group, or possibly by the IT compliance team. In many cases, the testing of a given set of controls is initiated by a compliance audit for a specific regulation. For example, an annual Sarbanes-Oxley Act (SOX) audit may trigger testing of controls that impact SOX compliance. A subsequent PCI audit may have the same effect, possibly resulting in the redundant testing of controls that relate to both SOX and PCI. This redundant testing of controls is caused by compliance silos—a lack of a centralized repository where all information about controls and their status is kept.

When a control fails, a remediation process is generally initiated in order to make the control match the requirements of the corporate policy. This remediation process may be very simple and straightforward, or in some cases could require a substantial IT project to correct them. This might involve assigning engineers to design, test, and document a fix.

Failed controls also impact the risk profile of the associated policy, and this risk needs to be communicated back to the policy owner so that it can be effectively handled. This is a common problem in many organizations that don't have a centralized repository of risk and compliance controls information. Let's assume that a given control is used for both PCI and SOX compliance. During the annual SOX audit, the control is tested and the error rate is determined to be higher than allowed by the associated policy. This control failure also impacts PCI compliance, possibly to an unacceptable level. But without a mechanism to communicate this information, or at least a central place where it is stored, the owner of the PCI compliance program now has an emerging risk that they are unaware of.

A Life-Cycle Example

Let's look at an example of a policy life cycle as depicted in Figure 3-3. Note that some boxes that were included in Figure 3-2 have been removed for readability.

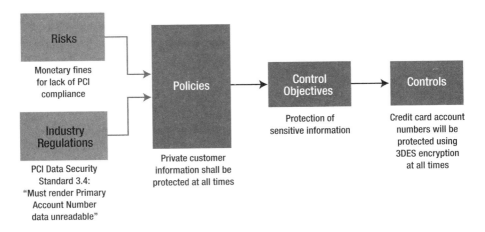

Figure 3-3. Policy life cycle example

Let's assume that your company processes credit card transactions, and therefore compliance with the PCI Data Security Standard (PCI DSS) regulation is a business requirement. The risk of noncompliance with PCI involves monetary fines. One of the requirements of the PCI DSS standard relates to the general statement that users' Primary Account Numbers must be unreadable.[1] This requirement is translated into a corporate policy and a series of control objectives are specified that indicate how you intend to conform to the policy. In essence, these control objectives will define the intent of a set of controls that you will implement. In this case, a specific control is designed that will encrypt all confidential customer account numbers with triple Data Encryption Standard encryption (3DES). As these controls are tested on an ongoing basis, inevitably failures will occur due to

---

[1] PCI Security Standards Council, PCI DSS, http://www.pcisecuritystandards.org https://www.pcisecuritystandards.org/security_standards/pci_dss.shtml (accessed 1 December 2009).

design deficiencies, unanticipated inputs, or the like. Any control failure should be corrected to help ensure compliance with policy, and retested on an ongoing basis.

Conclusion

This chapter highlighted the importance of a good policy-management infrastructure for the success of your governance activities. Policies dictate behavior that management wants to instill in their employees and partners and, when followed properly, help to ensure that the company meets its business objectives. When policies are not followed properly, detection and remediation of noncompliance is critical.

Risk Management

by Sumner Blount

Previous chapters have looked at the broad areas of governance and how these areas relate to each other. It's now time to focus on one of the most important areas of governance: the management of enterprise risk.

The Rise of Risk Management

Today's business world is dramatically more complex than in past years. The online availability of applications and data, the expansion of complex partner and supplier relationships, and the speed of today's economic changes mean that enterprises need to consider many more risks. In addition, risks are rarely self-contained; they're often related to each other in complex and hard-to-manage ways. A failure in one area of the business can have dramatic effects on other areas. A failure of business partners (or partners of business partners) may add significant risk to an organization.

A number of industry and market factors have increasingly caused the management of corporate risk to become a critical issue for business executives and Boards of Directors. First, the number and breadth of governmental regulations have increased significantly over the past few years. Second, increased globalization means that risk affects many more areas, across country boundaries, than ever before. Finally, the catastrophic (both financial and reputational) effects of some recent breaches of corporate security have increased the importance of effective risk management across all vertical markets, particularly financial services.

These factors are among the most important reasons that corporations are moving toward formal risk management programs and initiatives.

Elements of Successful ERM

Later in this chapter, we'll look at the phases of the risk management process and how they interact with each other. But first, let's consider some basic principles that all effective risk management models should embrace and follow. These characteristics cut across the stages of Enterprise Risk Management (ERM) and involve not only business processes but also people and organizational considerations:

- Assign a clear risk management process owner.

- Utilize a common risk management framework.

- Use industry best practices.

- Integrate risk management with business processes.

- Develop a culture of openness.

- Make it clear that risk management is "everyone's job."

Assign a Clear Risk Management Process Owner

Management of the *risk process* is one of the most important responsibilities in ERM. It's distinct from, but no less important than, managing the *risks* themselves. A single person, perhaps a Chief Risk Officer, needs to ultimately own the responsibility for the risk management process, from initial design to ongoing monitoring. Any business process that isn't monitored on an ongoing, continuous basis may deteriorate over time, and risk management is no exception. Deterioration of this process may have a dramatic impact on the business.

Utilize a Common Risk Management Framework

One of the most important characteristics of a mature risk environment is the presence of a *common risk management framework* across the enterprise. Sounds nice—but what does this mean? Simply that all the methods used for risk management throughout the organization are well-defined and communicated, consistent, and comprehensive. For example, you should identify risks through the use of a standardized, common risk library and terminology, so that all risks are categorized according to the same taxonomy. Risk assessments should be done using a common set of processes, including a centralized repository of risk-assessment documents and an automated workflow that enables the assessment to be done by the people on the front lines who have access to the best information related to the current state of the risk. And finally, you should use a set of common and well-defined measures to quantify the actual level of risk (likelihood, impact, inherent risk, residual risk, and so on), as well as mechanisms such as metrics and Key Risk Indicators (KRIs) to monitor the risk going forward on a continuous basis. In summary, a common risk management framework means that you identify, assess, measure, and monitor risks using the same basic terminology and processes across the organization.

A common risk management framework provides three important benefits to the organization. First, collaboration across groups improves because everybody has access to the same information and speaks the same language. Next, risk awareness and response are enhanced because risk monitoring can be automated and continuous, thereby alerting risk owners immediately when a given risk has exceeded defined thresholds and warrants remediation. Finally, overall risk decision-making is improved because information related to risks is accurate and timely, and can be presented in a way most suited to each person's needs.

Use Industry Best Practices

Many smart people in various industry organizations have put together industry best-practice models for managing risk across these industries. Take advantage of their work. It will not only save you time and help you avoid reinventing the wheel, but will also foster better communication across your organization and with your auditors. Because these models are generally recognized as industry best practices, convincing your auditors that you have an effective risk management environment in place will be easier if you have conformed to these established guidelines and practices.

The following are a few important industry frameworks to consider:

- *The ISACA Risk IT Framework*[1]: Provides a framework for enterprises to identify, govern, and manage IT risk, from the Information Systems Audit and Control Association (ISACA).

- *The ISO 27005 Standard for Information Security Risk Management*[2]: Provides guidelines for information security risk management in an organization, specifically supporting the requirements of an information security management system defined by ISO 27001.

- *The NIST Risk Management Framework*[3]: An approach to selecting security controls for information systems from the National Institute of Standards and Technology.

---

[1] Information Systems and Audit Control Association (ISACA), Risk IT, http://www.isaca.org/riskit (accessed 1 December 2009).

[2] International Standards Organization (ISO), ISO/IEC 27005 , http://www.iso.org http://www.iso.org/iso/iso_catalogue/catalogue_tc/catalogue_detail.htm?csnumber=4133 2 (accessed 1 December 2009).

[3] National Institute of Standards and Technology (NIST), NIST Risk Management Framework, http://www.nist.gov/groups/SMA/fisma/framework.html (accessed 1 December 2009).

- *The COSO Enterprise Risk Management-Integrated Framework*[4]: Provides guidelines for internal controls, from the Committee of Sponsoring Organizations (COSO).

- *The Australia/New Zealand (AS/NZS) Standard ISO 31000-2009 Risk Management*[5]: Defines risk management best practices.

- *The PCAOB Auditing Standard No. 5 (AS5)*[6]: Provides guidelines for auditors to assess risk of material misstatement in financial statements.

Integrate Risk Management with Business Processes

Risk management should not be an after-the-fact process that attempts to reduce the risk of a decision that has already been made. Rather, it should be part of the entire business process that leads to the decision. All participants along the various stages of a business process should be aware of the risk management activities that are required during each stage and should generate timely information for risk analysis that can be used by subsequent stages in the business process.

---

[4] Committee of Sponsoring Organizations of the Treadway Commission (COSO), "Enterprise Risk Management – Integrated Framework," 2004, http://www.coso.org/erm.htm (accessed 1 December 2009).

[5] Standards Australia, AS/NZS ISO 31000-2009 Risk Management – Principles and Guidelines, http://www.standards.org.au, http://infostore.saiglobal.com/store2/Details.aspx?ProductID=1378670 (accessed 1 December 2009).

[6] Public Company Accounting Oversight Board (PCAOB), Auditing Standard No. 5: An Audit of Internal Control Over Financial Reporting That Is Integrated with An Audit of Financial Statements, http://www.pcaobus.org/Standards/Standards_and_Related_Rules/Auditing_Standard_No.5.aspx (accessed 1 December 2009).

Develop a Culture of Openness

Risk-averse organizations often have limited communication about their current risk profile. Organizations that effectively manage risk tend to have cultures that are more tolerant of open communication and discussion related to risk.

It's natural that some people may feel a little vulnerable during a discussion about risks in their area of responsibility. Still, if communication about risk assessment or status isn't open and honest, bad things can happen. Moving to a culture of openness requires formal statements about expected behavior on the part of those involved in risk management, and executive management needs to lead and communicate by example.

Make It Clear That Risk Management Is "Everyone's Job"

Communication of risk strategies and goals must be consistent and widespread across the company. In order to succeed, an ERM program must be everyone's job at all levels. This implies three things. First, risk management needs to be an essential element of all critical business processes (described earlier). Second, everyone who plays a role in those processes must understand their role and its impact on risk management. And third, everyone who has a role in risk management as part of their responsibilities for a given business process needs to be measured on this area of responsibility. Telling someone that they have a role in risk management, but then not measuring them on it, doesn't provide an incentive for the behavior you want to instill.

The Risk Management Process: A Bird's-Eye View

Before we look at the details of how risk management can be done, let's identify some of the key roles in the risk management process, and attempt to define what we mean when we use the term "risk."

Risk Management Roles

Many different roles within the corporation need to be involved in the process of enterprise risk management. Someone (often the Chief Risk Officer) oversees the entire process to help ensure that risk management is consistent across all departments. Risk executives also need to effectively communicate the corporate risk tolerance, validate that employees understand how much risk they are allowed to undertake, and help ensure that this knowledge is being used to guide day-to-day risk-related behavior.

Centralizing risk information helps to ensure consistency of processes across the enterprise. It also allows executives to have visibility into the risk profile that the company has at any given point in time. This is essential because risks can change quickly, and remediation activities must keep pace.

Although risk information should be centralized, a specific risk is typically managed within the business unit that is impacted by that risk and is likely to be in the best position to monitor and manage the risk.

What Constitutes Risk?

Risk is a slippery term. Not only are there many, many different types of risk, but there are also many different opinions about what the term means. Risk is a function of four primary elements, expressed as follows:

RISK = f(ASSET, LOSS, THREAT, VULNERABILITY)[7]

Quantifying these variables in order to properly identify and assess a given risk is hard . . . very hard. First, doing so involves a lot of work across the organization to gather and classify information, with different groups often having widely differing views of these elements. Second, gathering the information is challenging—who do you solicit, how do you get the information, and how do you aggregate and consolidate it? And finally, as is

---

[7] RiskWatch, Inc., "Risk Assessment: Where Security Meets Compliance," http://www.riskwatch.com/RiskWatchWhitePapers.html (accessed 8 December 2009).

usually the case, there are often political challenges to arriving at a widely accepted model.

Despite the challenges, let's look at each of these elements to understand its relationship to risk:

- *Assets* are anything you need to protect. Assets include obvious things such as systems, applications, customer and corporate data, employees, physical buildings, and the like. They also include less tangible items such as your corporate reputation, your market position, and so on.

- *Loss* relates to the bad things that could happen to the *Asset*. Examples are direct theft, physical destruction, unauthorized disclosure, inappropriate modification, denial of service, or any other negative event.

- *Threat* includes any of the various ways that this *Loss* could occur. Examples are hackers, viruses, fraud, embezzlement, natural events, cyber attack, and the like.

- *Vulnerability* includes any weakness of your entire infrastructure. It's an aspect of your environment that could potentially contribute to the success of the *Threat*, resulting in the *Loss of the Asset*.

It's infinitely easier to describe this process than to engage in it. For example, generating a list of your assets is a fairly manageable task. But determining a specific value for the potential loss of any of those assets can be very hard. What is the potential loss, for example, resulting from the impact of a security breach on your corporate reputation?

Let's look at an example to see some of the items that can be included in each of these categories and how you can map them to each other to create a risk scenario. This model (based on material from RiskWatch, Inc.) identifies some examples for each category (Asset, Loss, Threat, Vulnerability) and creates a mapping that shows a set of *risk scenarios*. Each of these will be put into the risk management process (see the next section) for a complete analysis of each risk as depicted in Figure 4-1. The arrows in the diagram are examples; other scenarios are certainly possible.

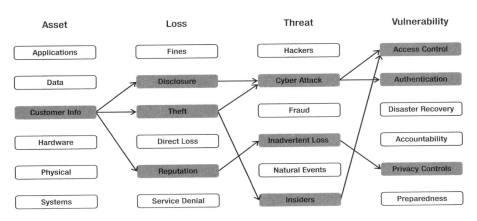

Figure 4-1. Sample risk scenario[8]

The Importance of Strategic Risk

The approach described in the previous section is an asset-based risk approach in that it focuses on corporate assets (even those that are intangible) and their associated risks. You could also take an objectives-based risk approach in which each strategic objective is analyzed in terms of the risks that negatively impact its attainment. This approach highlights areas of *strategic risk* to the corporation and is important because it uncovers areas that may preclude the success of your core business objectives.

Here is a simple example. Assume that your company has a primary manufacturing plant. There is a risk that this plant could burn down, so you take out insurance to compensate you in case that occurs. But it's likely that if the plant is destroyed, the cost will be the least of your worries. It may be the core of your business; if it's out of commission, your business may be in serious jeopardy. In that case, you must deal with a serious strategic risk, whether through backup manufacturing facilities, second-sourcing, or other means.

---

[8] RiskWatch, Inc., RiskWatch Analysis Engine, http://www.riskwatch.com (accessed 1 December 2009).

Only when you're able to easily associate (map) your risks to your policies and your strategic objectives will you be able to fully visualize the level of strategic risk that you have. As you plan your risk management approach, be sure to take advantage of technology solutions that make these associations visible across your entire environment.

Risk Management Process: Key Phases

Now that you've taken a bird's-eye look at risk, let's translate it into something more down to earth by looking at the activities that constitute the overall risk management process.

Risk management consists of a series of interrelated phases, as depicted in Figure 4-2. Think of this as a continuous feedback loop that is in constant operation and adjustment mode. The figure illustrates the major phases of risk management, but note that Monitor Risks is an ongoing, continuous process that can reinitiate any previous phase. An emerging risk discovered during the monitoring process may cause a reassessment of the risk, followed by a reprioritization, and so on. But it may also result in a modification of the top-level risk management policies established initially.

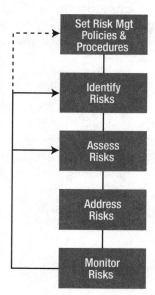

Figure 4-2. Phases of risk management

Let's look briefly at each of these major risk management phases.

Setting Risk Management Policies and Procedures

Executive management is responsible for establishing the framework of risk management within which all employees operate. They set the ground rules and articulate how much risk the organization is willing to take on. As seen from the financial crisis that emerged in 2008, merely stating the level of acceptable risk doesn't guarantee that it will be understood or followed.

Policies are broad statements of intent that management wants to follow. A policy might be, for example, "We will ensure that only people with a need to know will be able to access customer credit card information." Because a policy may not be specific enough to guide employee behavior in all cases, *procedures* (also called *standards*) may need to be established to define how the policy should be implemented. For example, a procedure might state that "All employee accounts will be disabled within one hour of the termination of that employee." The policy describes the end result that is desired, and the procedure describes behavior that contributes to meeting this end result.

Policies should address specific, identified risks, and therefore would be modified over time as these risks change in nature or importance.

Identifying Risks

Risk identification is the process of creating a list of the risks that you need to be aware of and potentially manage. Although it's often combined with risk assessment as a single process, we separate them here because they require different methods and practices and can be treated as two separate but highly related steps in your risk management process.

A key to good risk identification is a well-thought-out process to collect and filter initial risk information. It would be nice if all risks were obvious and could be easily entered into a repository. Unfortunately, this is rarely the case. Risks are often hard to identify, complex because they involve many forces interacting in unknown or unpredictable ways, and frequently made up of smaller risks that are localized within a single organization. Sometimes the true nature and severity of a risk are apparent only when the risk is viewed in the broad enterprise scope.

Techniques for Initial Risk Identification

You can obtain an initial list of risks through a number of different techniques:

- *Brainstorming*: Get knowledgeable people in a room to share their ideas on critical risks.

- *Surveys*: Conduct automated (or manual) surveys of individuals on the front lines to help identify risks that each person sees from their unique perspective.

- *Interviews*: Conduct detailed interviews with key individuals about risk as they see it.

- *Working groups*: Hold discussions with multiple groups of key people, generally focusing on a specific area of risk.

- *Industry analyst or thought leader output*: Search related articles or documents related to each area of risk.

- *Experience from previous projects*: Take advantage of experience that's available either directly from individuals or from project/program documents.

- *Industry best practices*: Many industry groups have produced lists of risks for certain areas, which can provide valuable information.

Risk Taxonomies and Libraries

The final step in risk identification is to classify each risk according to some naming convention. Reinventing the wheel here isn't a good idea. A number of industry firms and groups have put together risk taxonomies for certain areas of risk. For example, Standard & Poor's has published a draft list of risk categories as part of their ongoing effort to include risk management as part of their corporate evaluations.

In addition, a few companies offer risk libraries as a licensed component, often as part of a larger governance, risk, and compliance (GRC) management solution. Figure 4-3 illustrates a small subset of what such a risk library might contain. The figure shows only a portion of the hierarchy for *internal risks;* as the ellipses indicate, many of this tree's nodes aren't illustrated here. The point is simply to highlight a few of the *people risks* and how they fit into the large risk library.

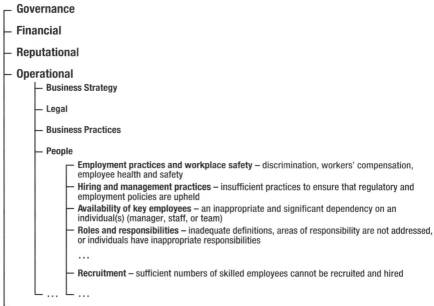

Figure 4-3. Sample risk library subset

Using an integrated risk library provides consistency across your organization in terms of how risks are described and classified, thereby helping to reduce confusion and improve communication.

Assessing Risks

Now comes the hard part. After you have identified the risks that you believe may impact the achievement of your business objectives, you need to assess their level of severity. Doing so involves two factors:

- *Risk likelihood*: How likely is it that this risk event may occur?

- *Risk impact*: If it does occur, what will be the overall impact on the organization?

These estimates are very difficult to arrive at with a high degree of confidence. Not only do individuals' estimates of these factors differ greatly within the same environment, but these factors also vary across industries, even for the same risk. As an extreme example, the risk likelihood and impact of severe weather are much different for a manufacturing company based in Key West, Florida, than for a financial institution on Wall Street.

The risk likelihood is often the hardest value to estimate. Information such as actuarial tables, weather history, and so on may be helpful. In general, however, this is an inexact science where intelligent people have to estimate the likelihood of an event that may never have occurred before, let alone in the recent past.

It's important to be specific in these estimates, but not *too* specific. For example, *low*, *medium*, and *high* aren't good measurements for risk likelihood, given that these terms can be interpreted in radically different ways. It's better to create a form of measurement, such as "will occur once every 5 years," to help ensure a semblance of consistency across estimates.

The chart in Figure 4-4 depicts a sample matrix on which you can graph your key risks.

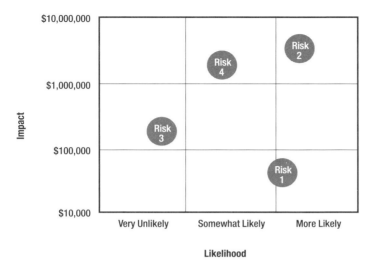

Figure 4-4. A risk assessment matrix

How can you determine the metrics you need to graph your risks? In a way that's similar to your risk identification process: with a combination of surveys, brainstorming, literature research, questionnaires, group discussions, and the like. When you have a baseline set of risk assessments (estimates), it's important to review them with a related peer group—the managers, professionals, IT people, and others who can provide useful input to the process. This not only helps to identify outlying opinions that are not shared widely but also serves to instill ownership of these risk estimates across the group of people who need to be aware of—and possibly manage—them.

The last step in risk assessment (many would argue that it should be a separate, independent step) is to prioritize the risks and assign owners for them. Prioritization is an important activity because sometimes how you address a risk isn't solely related to its likelihood and impact. For example, you may have temporary business constraints or budget issues that prevent you from addressing a given risk right now, at least in the way you would like to. Determine which risks you need to focus on, given all your existing constraints, and assign someone to address each such risk.

Make sure the business people impacted by a given risk drive its prioritization, even though someone outside the business may be assigned to manage the risk. To do this, you need to express the effect of all risks (including IT risks) in business terms—how they will impact not only the IT environment but, more important, the overall business.

Addressing Risks

At this point, you have generated a list of prioritized risks, with the estimated likelihood and impact of each risk on your overall business objectives. You now know which risks are the most important to deal with. The next step is to determine *how* to deal with each of them.

You can deal with any given risk in four main ways:

- Accept it.
- Transfer it.
- Mitigate it.
- Avoid it.

Risk acceptance is what the name implies—either the likelihood or the impact are low enough that you're willing to accept your fate if the risk event occurs. For example, the total costs to insure against or mitigate a small risk may be greater than the loss that would be incurred. Another example is a risk (such as war or insurrection) whose result would be so catastrophic that insurance or mitigation isn't feasible.

Risk transfer occurs when you pay a fee for someone (for example, an insurance company) to assume some or all of the risk for you. Risk transfer may reduce financial exposure, but may be insufficient for certain types of risks. For example, even if the loss of a manufacturing plant is covered financially, the event may have a catastrophic negative impact.

Risk mitigation is the typical business case. It involves the creation of *controls* to reduce the risk to an acceptable level (your risk tolerance). Examples of risk mitigation techniques vary widely and include access-control mechanisms, corporate policies that define acceptable laptop configurations, fire sprinklers, and employee proximity cards. Almost all risk mitigation approaches have tradeoffs, such as cost versus convenience, and it's often a complex balancing act to determine just how much protection is good enough.

Risk avoidance occurs when you don't undertake the activity that engenders the risk, thus eliminating the possibility of the negative outcome. Not entering a new business because of the risk, and not flying because you're afraid of a terrorist attack, are examples of risk avoidance. The problem, of course, is that avoiding risks means you also avoid the potential upside. If a business avoids all risks, it isn't likely to be in business very long. Avoidance is generally an appropriate response only for high-likelihood, high-impact events that could prove catastrophic.

Figure 4-5 illustrates some typical and reasonable approaches that you can apply to each area of the matrix from Figure 4-4. Note that these are really continuums rather than discrete boxes; therefore, they're only illustrative of which approaches may be most reasonable.

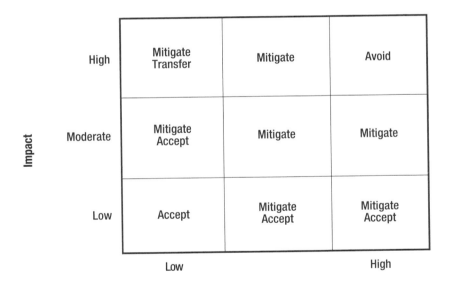

Figure 4-5. Common risk management approaches

Monitoring Risks

Now that you've assessed and prioritized your risks, and created a risk management plan for them, it's time to determine on an ongoing basis how that plan is working. Risks need to be monitored continuously in order to help ensure that your plan is effective and that no emerging risks affect your business.

But how do you monitor your risks? Staring at a risk dashboard all day may make you feel like you've got everything under control, but there are more effective ways to manage risk.

Make sure, as you learned earlier, that everyone involved in key business processes understands their impact on risk and the importance of reporting information or status that may also affect risk. Ideally, this involves direct input of data into a central repository so that the impact of the information on your risk profile can be instantly analyzed (this is an outgrowth of the common risk management framework discussed earlier). The goal is to ensure that people on the front lines can immediately report information relating to the status of risk mitigation controls, so that executive or management decisions are based on timely and accurate information.

But what type of information should you seek in order to help monitor risks? *Key Risk Indicators (KRIs)* are a commonly used metric. A KRI is a *leading indicator of an area of risk to business performance*. These metrics are simple, (ideally) easy to capture, and are useful predictors of downstream affects on the business. Some examples of KRIs include the turnover rate of key personnel, the number of system configuration changes over time, and the availability level of key IT services.

How can you measure effects on your business? Ultimately, the business boils down to revenue, profit, and other key financial metrics as reported in your annual report. But other, more immediate values generally are impacted before these critical metrics—sort of like the proverbial canary in the coal mine.

These values, called *Key Performance Indicators (KPIs)*, are *non-financial* leading indicators of business performance. If you wait until you experience a measureable impact on your key financial metrics (profit) before taking action, your ability to correct the problem in a timely way will be limited at best. Example KPIs include your rate of on-time delivery, rate of customer retention, quality of materials, and so on. Left unchecked, each of these could cause big changes in your financial performance.

Let's look at an example to illustrate this point. Suppose you define this KRI: "Turnover Rate of Key IT Administrators." If this rate increases significantly, it's likely that IT effectiveness will decrease. System downtime will probably go up, and partners and distributors will have trouble getting product information as needed or placing their orders. So, you can define the KPI "Partner Order Rate," which is the rate at which your partners' orders are coming in as compared to the historical average (see Figure 4-6).

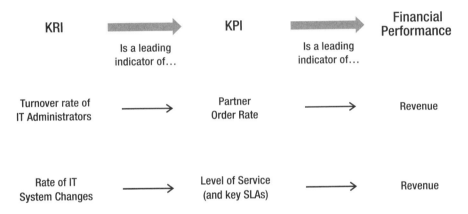

Figure 4-6. Using KRIs to monitor risk

Deriving these indicators, and making sure you understand the relationship between them, can be challenging. But if you're going to manage risk to your business effectively, you need to understand what factors will impact it and how you can identify trends before they become critical.

Conclusion

Risk management is one of the most important functions of a business and key to good governance. Effective risk management needs to permeate— and be an essential part of—all of the enterprise's critical business processes and strategic decisions. You only have to look at the recent financial crisis to see numerous examples of horrendous risk management decisions and oversights that had a catastrophic effect on companies, on the economy as a whole, and therefore on each one of us. More effective risk management, coupled with some anticipated regulatory changes and other governance improvements, may help prevent a recurrence. Similarly, improved enterprise risk management methods and practices can help ensure that your organization can more effectively meet its strategic business goals.

Risk Governance and the Board of Directors

by William E. McCracken

Something needs to change. There are good people in company management and good people on Boards of Directors. So why did the financial meltdown of 2008–2009 happen? One reason may be that some Boards didn't know enough about what was going on in their companies in general—in terms of risk governance in particular.

The Board of Directors should set high standards for a company's employees, officers, and Directors. Implicit in this philosophy is the importance of sound corporate governance. It is the duty of the Board of

Directors to serve as a prudent fiduciary for shareholders and to oversee the management of a company's business. Shareholders of a widely held public company are probably not aware of how the company's day-to-day operations are managed. They don't have visibility into every level of the business of the company. And they shouldn't be expected to. The Board of Directors is the shareholders' representative to company management. The Board's role is to govern the organization by setting strategic goals, adopting policies, and monitoring operations to try to ensure that management achieves the organization's objectives within guidelines established by the Board. The Board sets performance objectives with management, and management defines metrics for the Board to measure the organization's efforts toward reaching those objectives.

The Role of the Board as It Relates to Governance

Governance, culture, and what the company stands for need to start with the Board of Directors. The Directors should conduct their organization—that is, the Board—in such a way as to set an example for the rest of the company. The governance that they adhere to, and their dedication to looking at and doing the right things as a Board to help guide and protect the company and to grow the company for the shareholders, should all start in the boardroom. Therefore, Boards themselves should be conscious that they are, in fact, setting the standard for governance, the culture in the company, and the way it operates on a day-to-day basis. For all practical purposes, governance begins with the Board of Directors.

The Board and the Financial Crisis

The economic climate that surfaced in late 2008 resulted from the lack of both good governance and adequate risk oversight, underscoring that governance is a requirement that Boards and companies have to pay attention to. Not doing so gives us problems like those of the recent financial crisis. And these problems are a lot harder to fix than they would be to prevent.

Simply stated, if you don't pay attention to good governance, you run out of control.

Experience as a Catalyst for Change

A forum at the Millstein Center for Corporate Governance and Performance at Yale University's School of Management included discussions on the role of Boards in general and the role of Boards with respect to the financial meltdown in particular. We took a look at risk management, compensation practices, and shareholder protection. We talked about many of the things discussed in this chapter. Several people mentioned that we (CA's Board of Directors) have taken very aggressive action to achieve good governance. One person commented, "You've gone a long way on addressing governance. It might be hard for other organizations to go that far, but you had a near-death experience and that's why you went there." That is true. We did.

In 2004, CA entered into a Deferred Prosecution Agreement (DPA) that arose out of the criminal conduct of certain of the company's former executives relating to improper revenue recognition, and then obstructing the government's investigation of this practice.

An independent examiner was appointed to help CA identify and address all DPA issues and strengthen our internal controls and compliance. That launched a time of intense focus on governance, characterized by the company's demand for a high level of transparency, ethical behavior, and integrity from the entire organization. In successfully concluding the DPA, CA, guided by management, made great strides in putting in place the business systems, processes, and procedures to systematize governance and facilitate the company's ability to grow and generate value for shareholders, customers, and employees.

Clearly, we had a need for a heavy, concentrated focus on governance in the company. However, many of the innovative things that we've done, we did after we fulfilled our legal obligations under the DPA, including:

- Establishing and raising of the stature of the Chief Risk Officer

- Establishing the Compliance and Risk Committee of the Board

- Setting up the dual role reporting of the Chief Risk Officer both to the CEO (through the executive vice president of Risk and Administration) and to the Board (through the Compliance and Risk Committee)

Our experience heightened our awareness of how important good corporate governance is and how it must be part of the culture established at the Board level and pushed down through management to the entire organization.

We did have a daunting experience. But what company right now could argue that they have not? The market cap of the Fortune 1000 declined drastically during the 2008–2009 financial crisis. With the Dow Jones Industrial Average going down from over 14,000 to just over 6,000, many companies had their own perilous experiences. Who could argue that maintaining the status quo makes sense under these circumstances? Something needs to change, and improved governance can help bring about the change that's needed.

Evolution of Boards

The role of Boards is evolving over time. Ten or more years ago, Boards were less aware of their role in governance; circumstances then may not have required it. Boards would often review the information that management presented to them, agree or disagree, and provide input—but in some cases didn't consider themselves to be the starting point for good corporate governance, as many Boards do today.

We've seen examples, including with WorldCom and Enron, and more recently with financial organizations taking on too much risk, where the governance that emanated out of boardrooms was either inadequate or didn't make its way across the enterprise. Or both.

Boards have now seen the requirement and need—and shareholders are asking Boards to see the requirement and need—to be much more involved in governance. The information necessary to be able to properly protect the shareholders and the company should be the focus of what Boards think about. Therefore, that information should be both comprehensive and objective. Directors should have an open dialogue with management to understand in detail what is going on in the company.

Best Practices

Some corporations have responded to the increased scrutiny of corporate behavior with increased attention to governance. Fortunately, there are organizations that study and recommend best practices and provide a forum for discussing new policies and procedures and vetting ideas. One organization that I have been privileged to be involved with is the Millstein Center. Its website (millstein.som.yale.edu) contains invaluable information on tried-and-true best practices as well as potential best practices of the future.

The following are ten fundamental areas that Boards should pay attention to as corporate stewards. Some can be called best practices. Others are more leading-edge and subject to debate. Although they may not yet have achieved widespread adoption, these ideas could represent the wave of the future.

1. Ensure the Chairman-CEO Split

A trend that is developing in business is the splitting of the Chairman of the Board and CEO roles. In 2002, 22% of the Standard & Poor's 500 had divided the Chairman and CEO roles. Today, the figure is 37%. Outside the U.S., all German and Dutch companies divide the roles. In the U.K., about 79% of the companies report divided roles.[1] Many feel that split roles should now be the standard. Separation makes for good governance because it lessens the potential for a conflict of interest between the two roles and provides some measure of separation of powers and checks and balances. It changes how the CEO manages, not by impinging on the CEO's management responsibilities, but by having the Chairman help manage the Board's activities. Having the Chairman run the Board frees up the CEO to focus on running the business.

---

[1] Joann S. Lublin, "Chairman-CEO Split Gains Alliance: Corporate Leaders Push for Firms to Improve Oversight by Separating Roles," *Wall Street Journal*, 30 March 2009.

2. Utilize the Board's Experience

We should utilize the Board's experience to the fullest extent—just as we would any other valuable company asset. To take advantage of your experience, to take advantage of the mistakes you've made yourself, you need to have early warning systems. You need to have something that piques your attention, that puts your antennae up, that makes you want to know more about a subject.

If a presentation doesn't include an appropriate discussion of risks, the individuals sitting around the table may never say, "Wait a second, tell me more about that. Why do you believe that is going to work?"

The Board should know more about what is going on in the company. Some have recommended increasing the Directors' time commitments, perhaps even creating a new role of full-time "Professional Director."

3. Get over the "Directing vs. Managing" Conundrum

Some Boards have taken too strong a stance that they should be directing, not managing. This has caused some Directors to say, "If we question too much, if we dig down too far, we're moving into management, and that is not what we are here for. The managers and the executives are here to manage the company."

That's probably been taken to an extreme.

To go a level or two deep on a subject to truly understand what is going on, and to help management avoid risks and problems that may come up at a later point in time if ignored, you have to ask questions. Understanding what is going on in the company isn't managing the company. It's understanding the company. It's giving you the opportunity to take advantage of your experience as a Director to have input to management. It's your opportunity to say, "Watch out for this. I've been there. I ran into a buzz saw. This is what happened to me, and it could happen here. Maybe not. But be aware." That dialogue may stimulate other Directors to provide input as well, which is useful, beneficial, and helpful.

Business is as much, if not more, art rather than science. If it were science, lots of people would go to school, get an MBA, study how to run a business, and go back and run the business—and the business would be successful. We know that's not so. Businesses are not automatically successful. It doesn't matter what degrees you have. A lot of judgment and art go into the process of running a business. Combing through the detail of what is going on in the company is what encourages the dialogue during which that judgment and art are shared. We see the role of Boards evolving because the problems companies have experienced over the last couple of decades are catalysts for Boards to now focus more on what is going on. Having Directors obtain a significantly greater depth of understanding of the business is not usurping management. It is the Board members fulfilling their duty to understand what is going on and help management manage the company. The Board should let managers make decisions—and hold them accountable for those decisions—but should also have sufficient information to permit the meaningful examination of those decisions.

4. Leverage Your Committees, in General

The Board of Directors is typically organized into committees to provide focus, to allow members to specialize in a particular area of the company, and to take advantage of members' areas of expertise. The committees are based on major areas that the Board oversees, but the Board as a whole does not have the time collectively to get immersed in their detail. Committees are the eyes and ears of the Board of Directors. They have authority to fact-find, investigate, and ask tough questions of senior management as part of the Board's due diligence.

At CA, our committees are outlined in our "Corporate Governance Principles." This is a living document that provides an overarching map as to how our Board operates. For your convenience, this document can be found in Appendix A at the back of the book. The latest version is always available at ca.com under Investor Relations.

The CA Board has established the following committees to assist in discharging its responsibilities: the Audit Committee, the Compensation and Human Resources Committee, the Corporate Governance Committee, and the Compliance and Risk Committee. Almost all public companies have the first three committees, which are prescribed by the U.S. Securities and Exchange Commission and the national stock exchanges; but today very few companies have a Compliance and Risk Committee.

A. Audit Committee

The purpose of CA's Audit Committee is to assist the Board in fulfilling its oversight responsibilities with respect to

1. The audits of the Company's financial statements and the integrity of the Company's financial statements and internal controls;

2. The qualifications and independence of the Company's independent auditor (including the Committee's direct responsibility for the engagement of the independent auditor);

3. The performance of the Company's internal audit function and independent auditor;

4. The Company's accounting and financial reporting processes;

5. The activity of the Company's internal control function, including reviewing decisions with respect to scope, risk assessment, testing plans, and organizational structure; and

6. Accounting and financial compliance matters, in conjunction with the Compliance and Risk Committee.

Because we are focusing on risk governance in this chapter, it is important to note that the regulatory authorities typically assign the responsibility for risk oversight to the Audit Committee but generally permit that authority to be delegated by the Board to another committee. It is generally accepted that risk oversight should be assigned to a committee, and not necessarily to the Audit Committee. At CA, risk oversight, other than for financial reporting and accounting matters, is the domain of the Compliance and Risk Committee, to be described later in the chapter.

B. Compensation and Human Resources Committee

The Compensation and Human Resources Committee's purpose is to assist the Board in fulfilling its responsibilities with respect to executive compensation and human resources matters, including:

1. Reviewing and approving corporate goals and objectives relevant to the compensation of the CEO; in coordination with the Corporate Governance Committee, evaluating his or her performance in light of those goals and objectives; and determining and approving his or her compensation based upon such evaluation; and

2. Determining the compensation of senior executives other than the CEO, including determinations regarding equity-based and other incentive compensation awards.

C. Corporate Governance Committee

The Corporate Governance Committee's purpose is to assist the Board in fulfilling its responsibilities with respect to the governance of the Company, and includes making recommendations to the Board concerning:

1. The size and composition of the Board, the qualifications and independence of the Directors, and the recruitment and selection of individuals to stand for election as Directors;

2. The organization and operation of the Board, including the nature, size, and composition of Committees, the designation of Committee Chairs, the designation of a Lead Independent Director, Chairman of the Board or similar position, and the process for distribution of information to the Board and its Committees; and

3. The compensation of non-employee Directors.

At first glance, it may seem that the Corporate Governance Committee would be the committee emphasized in a book on governance. However, as described earlier, the Corporate Governance Committee is more concerned with the operation and governance of the Board. It is the

Compliance and Risk Committee described next that is more central to the governance theme of this book.

D. Compliance and Risk Committee

According to the "Corporate Governance Principles," the Compliance and Risk Committee's general purposes are:

1. To provide general oversight to the Company's enterprise risk management and compliance functions;

2. To provide input to management in the identification, assessment and mitigation of enterprise-wide risks faced by the Company both internally and externally; and

3. To provide recommendations to the Board with respect to its review of the Company's business practices and compliance activities and enterprise risk management.

Because of this chapter's emphasis on risk governance, an expanded discussion of the Compliance and Risk Committee is included in the next section.

5. Leverage the Compliance and Risk Committee, in Particular

Why do bad things happen to seemingly well-run companies? How do you prevent them from happening? These questions were largely the impetus behind the creation of the Compliance and Risk Committee by our Board. We did not have, and most Boards do not have, a committee that focuses primarily on enterprise risk management.

Let's focus on two of the Compliance and Risk Committee's main responsibilities. The *first* is to give order, discipline, and thought to how we process information that has to do with risk. How does the Board establish a risk appetite as it relates to the company's strategy, business operations, financial reporting, and legal and regulatory affairs? How do we decide which are the significant risks that the full Board needs to focus on with management?

After we have identified significant risks and related priorities, the *second* responsibility of the Compliance and Risk Committee is to deliver risk-related information to the Board. Without the Compliance and Risk Committee to set an appropriate agenda, it would be ad hoc as to how risk-related matters would come forward for discussion by the Board. The Compliance and Risk Committee puts discipline and order around the information that is given to the Board and provides, as other committees on the Board do, an opportunity to have a thoughtful agenda of topics that are focused on in a standard and recurring way.

By establishing a separate Compliance and Risk Committee, we are sending a clear message that these areas are extremely important to the organization.

Charters specify how committees are organized and how they operate. They are living documents and serve to document important Board responsibilities. The charter of the Compliance and Risk Committee can be found in Appendix B at the back of this book. The latest versions of CA's charters can be found on our website at http://www.ca.com under Investor Relations.

6. Create the Role of the Chief Risk Officer

The Board looks to management for risk information, and a key conduit of that information is the Chief Risk Officer. By working with the Compliance and Risk Committee, the Chief Risk Officer is a primary input into governance.

At CA, we have elevated the position of Chief Risk Officer so that the Chief Risk Officer has a dual reporting structure, reporting both to the CEO (through the executive vice president, Risk and Administration) and to the Board (through the Compliance and Risk Committee). It is a very significant position with senior management stature.

The role comprises two main responsibilities. *First*, it has the responsibility to work with business operations across the company. The Chief Risk

Officer needs to educate various groups on what Enterprise Risk Management is all about and then collaborate with them to identify risks in their areas and determine what mitigation steps, if any, are needed to bring their level of risk within the company's appetite for risk in those areas.

Risk is not a bad thing. Risk is a necessary part of running the business. You have to take risks to compete in any business.

The management of that risk—meaning identifying what those risks are and then deciding what to do as a result of understanding those risks—is what's important. For example, we may need to implement a new process or procedure, say a new worldwide sales process. Is that risky? Of course. It's risky because it's changing the operational mode that all the people who sell for us day-to-day have been using. If the implementation is not done effectively, efficiently, and appropriately, it could interrupt the sales cycle. If it interrupts the sales cycle, it interrupts the performance of the company in a given quarter or a given year.

Identifying that risk is important because after the risk is identified, the affected organization, in this case the Sales organization, can ask, "What are some of the things we need to do to mitigate that risk and avoid having an interruption to the sales cycle?" As long as it is handled in a disciplined manner, risk is not a negative thing. It is a necessary part of the way you run a business.

The *second* main responsibility of the Chief Risk Officer is to report risk information to the Board through the Compliance and Risk Committee. The Chief Risk Officer is one of the principal conduits of risk information to the Board, providing an additional candid assessment that the Board needs to engage in the enterprise risk management aspect of good governance.

The Compliance and Risk Committee works closely with the Chief Risk Officer to identify the areas of significant risks that need to be reported on. It's a two-way street. The Chief Risk Officer provides valuable information to the committee based upon his or her observations and discussions with management concerning significant risks. The committee members provide valuable information back to the Chief Risk Officer based on their knowledge of the company and their extensive experience. With this input from the committee, the Chief Risk Officer is empowered to facilitate risk management with the direction and backing of the committee.

The fact that the Chief Risk Officer's input into the Board is candid and direct is of the utmost importance. Board members with any experience running a company of any size understand that no company runs perfectly all day, every day. Doesn't happen. Can't happen. Won't happen. Therefore, to think that if you take a problem to a Board, the Directors are going to say, "You're out of control," is not so. It's far better to flag problems and then discuss and debate what you are going to do about those problems, than to not identify those problems at all.

For example, it was recounted that a large financial management firm had a risk officer who started blowing the whistle 18 months before the collateralized debt obligations (CDOs) came crashing down in the financial area. That risk officer was dismissed from the company. Looking back, if that company had debated those risks, discussed how those risks could affect the company, and looked at what they could do to eliminate some of those risks, there might have been a very different outcome. That is why in our company, it is the Chief Risk Officer's responsibility to identify risks to the Compliance and Risk Committee members so that they can engage in discussions and debates about what should be done.

7. Standardize Your Risk Framework

Our Board spent significant time with management going over long-term strategy. As a result of that exercise, the company adopted, and the Board approved, a comprehensive strategy for the company to succeed in the future. The Board asked the Chief Risk Officer to facilitate bringing together information that it could look at on a standard basis to help track our progress in the execution of that strategy as well as our performance with respect to that execution.

The Chief Risk Officer worked with management to determine the metrics that would be most valuable in tracking the strategy implementation. The selected metrics cover both the project timeline (are we on schedule?) and the project scope (are we implementing what we said we were going to implement?). The set of management-owned metrics is vital input into the

Board's discovery process and serves to not only measure progress but also prompt focused discussion and to identify risks.

In order to make risk management a strategic element of your key business processes and decision-making, it is important to use it not only to help manage risks of a decision that has already been made, but also to incorporate risk management processes into the analysis of new business opportunities. Attention to which risks to avoid is as important as attention to which risks to take.

The Chief Risk Officer helps promote a strategic approach to risk management by encouraging the adoption of a common risk management framework across the enterprise. This includes uniform risk identification, terminology, assessment processes, and metrics. When everyone uses the same risk framework, they speak the same "language" and identify and assess risks in a consistent way, thereby improving collaboration, risk awareness and assessment, and decision-making. A common risk framework helps you align all your risk management activities with corporate strategy and objectives.

By championing the risk management framework, the Chief Risk Officer gives business operations the means to self-assess their risks according to agreed upon guidelines.

8. Watch How You Pass the [Risk] Baton

At a recent Compliance and Risk Committee meeting, we spent a lot of time talking about the tendency to look at risk *within* particular departments such as Sales, Finance, Legal, Business Practices, and others. However, we believe that most risk comes into play from the intersection of those organizations—during the handoffs from one to the other. One group may think that they have sufficiently handed off a process, whereas the receiving group is oblivious to the fact that previously undisclosed but important elements are missing.

Focus is needed on the risk that becomes inherent in our operations when we hand things off horizontally, between organizations. For example, many organizations, including Pricing, Finance, Legal, Sales, Marketing, and Business Practices, get involved when we do a contract renewal. The handoff between all of those organizations is critical to how well we perform that process, because each handoff has the potential to introduce risk. It's like passing a baton in a relay race. Most of the risk is introduced when the runners hand the baton from one person to another. If you drop it, you cannot win.

9. Build a Culture of Compliance

Part of good governance includes ensuring an ethical environment that encourages compliance with internal policies and external regulations. In fact, the Federal Sentencing Guidelines, which have been incorporated into prosecutorial guidelines of the Department of Justice, specifically require corporations to "promote an organizational culture that encourages ethical conduct and a commitment to compliance with the law."[2]

At CA, to help create such an environment, we published a Code of Conduct and annually ask employees to affirm that they understand it by completing a written attestation. In addition, we try to regularly raise their level of understanding of the Code by having them watch an online video or take computer-based training. The Code of Conduct goes beyond something we distribute every year so that we get a check mark in the box. It needs to be part of our culture. We're respectful of each other and of our customers. We do things with a high degree of integrity. There are guidelines, internal policies, and external regulations that drive some of the things that are in the Code of Conduct. Those need to be the foundation of our culture. People need to understand them, believe in them, and act on them in everything they do each day.

---

[2] U.S. Sentencing Commission, "2009 Federal Sentencing Guidelines Manual," 1 November 2009, http://www.ussc.gov/2009guid/tabcon09.htm (accessed 1 December 2009).

10. Assess Board Performance

On an annual basis, the CA Board assesses its performance against our published "Corporate Governance Principles" as well as against each of our committee charters. This is an opportunity for the Directors to reflect on the thoroughness of their knowledge of company. Are we doing what we said we were going to do? Are we doing it well? If we are not doing it, does it need to get done, or do our objectives need to change? If we need to do it, do we have processes and measurements in place to make it happen? Self-assessments are valuable at both the Board and Committee levels. In addition, there may be value in providing coaching for individual Directors to encourage a consistently effective level of participation and interaction by all Directors.

Assessments in general are an invaluable means to improvement, and regulatory authorities have recognized their importance. In fact, assessments of internal controls are mandated by the Sarbanes-Oxley Act of 2002 and SEC regulations.

Conclusion

According to John P. Kotter of the Harvard Business School and author of *Leading Change*, a crisis can be seen as positive in that it garners support for long-overdue change. Crisis brings with it opportunity and is a catalyst of change.[3]

The 2008-2009 economic environment is such a crisis—one exacerbated by the currently-developing complex interconnectedness of today's businesses, industries, and economies. Now is the time for companies and their Boards to step up and make meaningful changes in the way they address governance.

---

[3] John P. Kotter, *Leading Change*, Harvard Business School Press, 1996

To encourage reflection, dialogue, and action, this chapter purposely sets forth some controversial ideas for changes in how Boards address governance. The time is ripe for change. It is legitimate to discuss and debate what those changes should be, but it is very, very difficult to debate that changes are not called for.

Governance of Risk and Compliance

by Robert Cirabisi and Kenneth V. Handal

Every organization is exposed to events that have some likelihood of adversely impacting its objectives. This exposure includes laws and regulations—such as the Foreign Corrupt Practices Act (FCPA) and privacy regulations—that can result in significant consequences to a business. Proper management of, for example, relationships with vendors, customers, or other third parties, and of confidential information of employees and third parties, is required to avoid risk of fines and penalties. This is a common view of risk—one that is very much focused on compliance with laws and regulations.

In order to mitigate these risks, organizations perform governance activities that define policies and procedures and establish a culture of compliance. Best-in-class companies supplement these activities with education and training. Collectively, these activities encompass a typical risk-management profile that seeks to identify and optimize ways to address compliance risks. Management of compliance risk has taken on a much greater role since the historic corporate failures that resulted in the enactment of the Sarbanes-Oxley Act (SOX) of 2002.

The Federal Sentencing Guidelines in U.S.S.G. Section 8B2.1 require that, to have an effective compliance and ethics program, an organization must:

> *"Exercise due diligence to prevent and detect criminal conduct"*

and

> *"Otherwise promote an organizational culture that encourages ethical conduct and commitment to compliance with the law."* [1]

The Guidelines further provide that:

> *"Such compliance and ethics program shall be reasonably designed, implemented, and enforced so that the program is generally effective in preventing and detecting criminal conduct."* [2]

Partially in response to these Guidelines, as well as other guidance relating to the prosecution of organizations, companies have been putting a lot of time and resources into sustaining this function and creating a compliance view of risk.

---

[1] U.S. Sentencing Commission, "2009 Federal Sentencing Guidelines Manual," 1 November 2009, http://www.ussc.gov/2009guid/tabcon09.htm (accessed 1 December 2009).

[2] http://www.ussc.gov/2009guid/tabcon09.htm.

However, for all the resources invested in compliance activities, such matters represent only a portion of the risks faced by organizations and only part of an organization's potential value destructors.

In Chapter 2, risk was defined as "a measure of the impact of uncertainty on the achievement of business goals." Risks impact a broad spectrum of business objectives, such as strategic, operational, financial, legal, and regulatory objectives. Risk management is the process by which an organization sets its risk tolerance, identifies potential risks, and prioritizes its tolerance for risk based on business objectives. The goal of risk management is to reduce loss (due to negative risk) and to create value for the company (through prudent risk-taking).

How are organizations managing risks? As we've said previously in this book, many companies today manage risk and compliance within silos, with each silo focused on its own world of risk management. Some companies think of risk management as a legal, treasury or finance role, each of which focus on very discrete aspects of risk. For example, an insurance company may think of its claims reporting and accounting as the core of its risk management function.

Indeed, many treasury professionals have "risk manager" in their titles; but for the most part, they're looking at the company's insurable risks.

Reporting structures may add complexity to risk management. In some companies, corporate compliance reports to legal. Corporate strategy may report to the CEO or CFO, and internal audit or financial controls may report to another group. The ability to work together and to communicate effectively about the company's risk and risk responses across departments can be a challenge. One team may own the policy, another may own the training, and another the business operation. In many cases, there is overlap, which can lead to multiple departments taking ownership and stepping on each other—or, worse, each department thinking the other is responsible (or vice versa).

Financial institutions implement highly sophisticated risk-management functions in their separate business groups. Where some financial institutions went wrong in the financial crisis that emerged in late 2008 is subject to much debate. Many questions abound as to whether the banks fully understood the risks of the financial products they were entering into and the broader impact to the organization. Moreover, it's unclear how transparent these risks were to the leaders of the organizations and their Boards of Directors, and whether these investments were truly consistent with the companies' investment philosophy and business strategy. Perhaps they over-relied on the fact that their organizations were making money and so assumed that all must be right with the world. One thing that is clear is that the risks were real and weren't managed sufficiently.

What's to be learned from this? There is no simple answer. As businesses grow more complex, managing risk holistically becomes more important but harder to accomplish. However, good governance in the form of an infrastructure that approaches risk on an enterprise-wide (not siloed) basis can improve your odds.

Organizing for Risk

Let's acknowledge that there is no one correct answer for a perfect risk-governance structure. What works for one company may not make sense for another. However, assuming the existence of appropriate resources and scale, a good, and perhaps even innovative, structure involves creating a real or virtual governance, risk, and compliance (GRC) team. This team's basic function is to look out over the whole organization to assess its risk management activities from both an operational and strategic point of view, within the context of enterprise risk management.

This team may include the disciplines of compliance, internal audit, financial controls (the group responsible for managing a company's SOX annual assessment), governance, and security. Team members may all report up to the Chief Compliance Officer, the Chief Risk Officer, or another executive. Or, groups within the team may report up to different executives. The actual org chart is less important than the fact that each team member is part of a cohesive enterprise-wide risk management effort.

The GRC team enhances communications, shares resources, and works with business groups as a unified entity while providing the tools and methodology needed to address risk in a consistent manner. This team approach overcomes the silo challenges; promotes ethical behavior and governance practices; and identifies, assesses, and monitors risks to accelerate risk-intelligent decisions while protecting the organization and, ultimately, shareholder value.

This centralized team structure can help to break down the silos that exist within the organization that prevent management from seeing the big picture. Team members look for trends across business functions and for areas where cross-functional dependencies exist. They ask questions such as: "How does that work?", "Can you explain the basis for that transaction?", and "How well-equipped is the company to manage the risks related to this opportunity?" They may not be popular as they question decisions throughout the organization, but they provide an objective view of risk for management and the Board of Directors as they conduct their governance responsibilities over the organization.

The GRC team looks to see what risks are looming and then works to help ensure that those risks are understood by management, managed properly, and, as appropriate, reported to the executive team or the Board of Directors. Providing this insight enables the team's collective wisdom and experience to help ensure that important issues are identified and addressed in a timely fashion. You want to avoid a major risk event occurring and the Board asking management "Why weren't we fully aware of this risk?" Not only should the Board of Directors be aware of the most critical risks impacting the company, but they should also have a good idea as to how those risks are being managed.

In our experience, managers at all levels are typically risk-aware and can quickly identify risks when asked a question such as, "What keeps you up at night?" However, they don't always effectively articulate the risk in the context of business objectives (for example, risk to what?), the likelihood of the risk occurring, or, more important, how significant that risk is to the organization. When interviewing managers, you may find that different views exist about what the top risks are, or that managers are quick to point out the significant risks to the company that exist in *other* departments. Views on risk can be highly subjective and may result in an inappropriate level of focus on the wrong areas at the expense of areas of higher risk.

The GRC team provides independent support to management by prioritizing the risks they should be focused on and the approaches that should be taken to mitigate these risks. Such prioritization should be based on a common view of how to measure risks, under the framework of a formalized enterprise risk management program.

The Committee of Sponsoring Organizations of the Treadway Commission (COSO) defines Enterprise Risk Management (ERM) as "a process, effected by an entity's board of directors, management and other personnel, applied in strategy setting and across the enterprise, designed to identify potential events that may affect the entity, and manage risk to be within its risk appetite, to provide assurance regarding the achievement of an entity's objectives."[3]

Very simply, ERM is a structured, consistent, and continuous risk management process applied across the entire organization. It provides a framework and methodology so that management can view and measure risk. For example, if you're unable to innovate to keep up with market changes, will that have a catastrophic or significant effect on your ability to survive? What does *catastrophic* mean in your organization? Additionally, what is the risk appetite of management and the Board of Directors with regard to such risk? And what do you have to do to respond to the risk? Your conclusions will still have some level of subjectivity, but ERM provides the framework to answer such questions relative to the organization and achieve management consensus on a prioritized risk response.

Partnering with the Business

Ironically, the GRC team needs to ensure that it doesn't become its own silo, reaching conclusions about risks to the business without performing an adequate level of due diligence and vetting within the organization. Cooperation from the business is needed to allow GRC team members to access information, meetings, and people so they can become knowledgeable business partners.

---

[3] Committee of Sponsoring Organizations of the Treadway Commission (COSO), "Enterprise Risk Management – Integrated Framework," 2004, http://www.coso.org/erm.htm (accessed 1 December 2009).

This partnership should entail proactive involvement with the business. Providing assessments after decisions are made or transactions are entered into doesn't optimize the value of the team to the business. For example, the team shouldn't wait for the company's strategy to be developed and implemented before generating a list of risks associated with that strategy. They shouldn't wait for a new policy to be established and then comment on it after the fact. They shouldn't look at major transactions or investments only after they're completed and then comment on the associated risks. Instead, the team should work with the business on a proactive basis throughout the decision-making process.

For example, the team should work closely with each business unit that has input into the organization's strategic plan to understand their strategic objectives and the key dependencies and risks associated with that portion of the company's strategy. Business unit management teams are extremely forthcoming when it comes to discussing the risks inherent in their plans. It gives them a sense of relief to air their risks and concerns and to talk about what they're doing to address these issues on one hand, and where they need help on the other.

The GRC team should partner by being proactive about major activities in the planning stages to understand project plans, business requirements, interdependencies, and the potential risks associated with implementations. We've seen the likelihood of risk rise significantly when implementing change; for example, new systems that create policies and processes with a high degree of cross-functional involvement. Ideally, GRC team members can challenge the business and provide valuable recommendations on control considerations, as well as assess whether risk management over the activity is adequate. Additionally, they should verify that appropriate constituents (such as finance, legal, IT, tax, and human resources) are involved.

To enhance the value they bring to the business, the team can provide risk assessment tools, guidance, and training with respect to risk and compliance activities. Training can range from general awareness training about compliance issues and enterprise risk management training for employees within business functions, to providing specific training for designated individuals (embedded resources) within the business functions. These embedded resources are tasked with the responsibility of monitoring compliance issues and risks and then working through assessment and response with management and the GRC team. Having embedded resources provides a foundation on which to build effective and knowledgeable communication, because such individuals can help translate business matters in the context of compliance or related risks.

This training and partnership is extremely useful when you're assessing potential risks, sometimes referred to as "emerging risks," as a result of activities elsewhere within the organization or in the external environment. All too often, we hear management tell compliance or risk-management groups, "Don't tell me about the risks I know about, tell me about the ones I don't know about." A challenge indeed—but the GRC team should proactively monitor the ever-changing internal and external environments to assess where the next shoe will drop.

As noted earlier regarding the financial crisis that began in 2008, how well some financial institutions understood the risks related to the transactions they entered into isn't clear, even with the use of highly sophisticated financial models. But these tools were used to manage risk at a very detailed level, perhaps only for the business unit, versus enterprise-wide. The transactions of one business unit can potentially jeopardize the survival of the overall organization, even when most of the other business units appear to be healthy. Companies need to be proactive in order to facilitate the management of risk at a much higher level. They must evaluate how risks affect the enterprise, not just the business unit, by consistently applying a relevant risk assessment methodology and using ERM to help management assess the impact of risk to the enterprise. This facilitates transparency and proper escalation.

Aligning the Organization for an Integrated Approach to Risk

You can achieve an inherent synergy by having a centralized GRC team to help ensure formalized, consistent, and prioritized communication of GRC activities. This is in stark contrast to a decentralized function that runs the risk of reporting risks and compliance activities to management and the Board of Directors in an unfiltered and haphazard manner that may fail to appropriately draw attention to the most pressing issues.

Resources should be aligned across the entire organization to achieve a streamlined and integrated risk function. This differs from an approach where, for example, each time a new regulation is enacted, a new regulatory silo is created, adding yet another layer and expense to the organization. If a regulation affects five or six groups within an organization, which is often the case, another five or six silos may result. The GRC team may be in a better position than business units to apply expertise to a problem and can always ask for help if they have issues requiring additional expertise.

For example, if the Sales team wants to provide training for new hires, they can reach out to the GRC team to help coordinate creation of a training program that encompasses things like legal and regulatory issues, and basic code-of-conduct training.

Similarly, if compliance issues or risks are evolving, the GRC team and the business units need to be aligned and integrated in order to address issues before they become major problems. Another example may be a major acquisition or divestiture. Clearly, inherent risks are associated with these types of activities—risks in terms of execution as well as impact on business strategy. A fully integrated GRC function helps ensure that you develop a comprehensive risk analysis of the associated transaction. In the case of an acquisition, an integrated view of risk helps ensure, among other things, that you undertake a robust analysis of your current business processes, information sources, and infrastructure, and align these with your acquisition target in order to develop a gap analysis. This, in turn, results in a more comprehensive plan to address integration challenges. Again, this process should be owned by the teams responsible for business development, with an integrated approach to risk facilitated by the GRC team to help ensure that critical issues rise to the top.

Developing a Holistic Vision of Controls Monitoring and Reporting

Thus far, we've talked about the benefits of a centralized risk and compliance function from a structure and process perspective. However, this discussion would be incomplete without a broader vision of how to effectively bring all these functions together using a common system.

Organizations should think about how all of their controls, policies, and compliance regulations interact. In many cases, if a company created an inventory, it would find that it was using scores of different applications and spreadsheets, with no consistent method to integrate them to help ensure there were no gaps or to eliminate redundancies. Many companies have created a hodgepodge of controls, policies, and regulations databases. Information is passed around by email and updated by each group according to its own needs. Over time, this situation gets worse, leading to the following:

- Duplication of information and/or inconsistent (and therefore incorrect) information.

- Duplication of effort. Different groups perform compliance activities (such as testing a control) that have already been done by another group.

- Lack of automation. Manual processes lead to high cost, delays, and sometimes costly errors.

- Lack of visibility. The lack of a "single source of truth" means that it's very hard to determine the exact state of compliance. In addition, the risks associated with compliance aren't visible, so the total corporate risk profile is difficult to determine.

For example, think of computer access control as a key business requirement. Access control is important for the folks doing SOX testing who have documented controls, policies, and testing processes for access to IT systems. If the organization processes data for customers using credit card data, PCI (Payment Card Industry) standards require that you have adequate controls over access to customer-related applications. You may be subject to HIPAA (Health Insurance Portability and Accountability Act) requirements and have people in charge of ensuring adequate access controls over patient data. If not properly managed, a scenario like this can result in various parties performing their own access-control risk assessments, creating documentation, and testing the same underlying applications!

A holistic management scheme for GRC may utilize technology to bring together these previously disparate functions, processes, databases, and applications into one enterprise-wide application. With technology, policies and controls can be aligned with business requirements and regulations, and the associated risks, testing plans, results, and action items can be centralized.

At CA, using our own CA GRC Manager software solution, we've created a centralized repository of policies and controls, which helps eliminate the duplication of information and reduces the risk of inconsistent or incorrect information being communicated to the organization about such policies and controls. We began using it to manage our SOX program for both IT and non-IT controls. The tool has allowed us to put all of our controls in one place, perform risk assessments, document our testing and related results, and summarize our results for effective follow-up, remediation, and reporting to management. Having this centralized tool has enabled us to achieve substantial savings by reducing the number of controls tested and the cost of testing each control.

Our vision for holistic controls monitoring and reporting extends further. First, we plan to centralize all of the company's policies, procedures, controls, and compliance and other regulatory requirements into CA GRC Manager. Next, we expect to create a common mapping of all interdependent sources of data using the tools within the GRC application. This step would enable us to eliminate redundancies and identify gaps in controls. Then, we would be able to link our controls and policies to the associated risks, forming the foundation for our ERM program.

Our objective is to use CA GRC Manager to enable control self-assessments for virtually every department at the company, and to facilitate the framework for continuous controls monitoring. The goal is to centralize and systematize GRC. This will lay the groundwork to enable much more efficient and effective SOX, internal audit, ISO quality, compliance, and enterprise-risk functions. What would it mean to a Chief Financial Officer or Chief Risk Officer to have all of a company's risks and controls in one place, enabling a single view of the risk environment? What would it mean to the head of internal audit to have a company's controls, policies, and procedures in a single repository, enabling you to create your audit program, perform your testing, and create a status of open findings from a single application? What would it mean to a Chief Compliance Officer to have all compliance functions (HIPAA, FCPA, lobbying activity, and so on) in a single place, enabling you to efficiently manage and report on these activities?

Finally, a discussion of this centralized view of risk and compliance wouldn't be complete without a mention of how you report your activities. Using a tool like CA GRC Manager lets you create an executive dashboard where, at a glance, senior management can see where the organization is positioned with respect to its risks and make risk-intelligent decisions. Senior management can then drill down at different levels to examine problems more closely. For example, the CFO can easily determine how many internal audit or SOX findings are open at any point in time. What's more, he or she can click on the finding and determine the details behind it, including the owner and the plan for remediation. The Chief Compliance Officer may want to see the number of instances of noncompliance, or open compliance issues.

Executive and Board Involvement

The GRC team will be successful only when it gets all the business functions to play on the same field at the same time. To accomplish this, the GRC team needs proper backing from the highest levels of the organization, including the Board of Directors. For example, suppose the GRC team asks to meet with executive management to understand the company's corporate merger and acquisition (M&A) strategy and the associated risks. Without backing from the highest levels, this request will likely be met with resistance. People have a natural tendency to feel second-guessed when you start asking questions. In addition, they don't want to invest time and energy working on something if they don't understand how it fits into the big picture of the company's success. If you can tell the M&A team that the company's ability to do successful acquisitions concerns the Board of Directors from a risk and compliance perspective, and the Board would like to understand the M&A risk-mitigation strategy, this will go a long way toward gaining cooperation.

A good way to help ensure backing from the highest levels is to create a committee of the Board of Directors that is responsible for compliance and risk and that the GRC team reports to on a dotted-line basis. Many companies assign this function to the Audit Committee; but considering the already-extended agendas and stress on that committee, creating a separate committee makes a lot of sense. The Board's GRC (or Compliance and Risk) Committee can help set the agenda for the GRC team, prioritize its efforts, and help establish the company's risk appetite. Figure 6-1 depicts the GRC team's reporting structure.

Figure 6-1. The company from a GRC team reporting perspective

Making it clear that the team has the backing of the Board provides several distinct benefits:

1. It shows how serious the company is about managing its risk and compliance program.

2. It helps ensure that the team knows what's important to the Board and avoids floundering and becoming bureaucratic.

3. It provides a vehicle to inform the Board without any filtering of the true risks and underlying root causes. The Board gains direct insight into the culture of integrity and a more substantive understanding of the most significant risk exposures at the organization.

Conclusion

As we stated in the beginning of this chapter, there is no correct answer as to the best structure for the governance of risk and compliance. It depends on your company's size, sophistication, business model, risk appetite, and other factors. However, unifying the governance of risk and compliance into a single function performed by a unified team clearly has its benefits. It enables you to provide tools, taxonomy, training, and guidance in a consistent and orderly manner. It lets you partner with the business to proactively address risks, challenge your risk assessments, and help ensure there are no gaps. Perhaps most important, it facilitates a consolidated view of risks for executive management and the Board of Directors, so that they can efficiently and effectively carry out their responsibilities to manage risk.

IT Governance, Risk, and Compliance

by Rob Zanella

Inevitably, as companies strive to achieve more effective governance, the focus turns to IT. With computer systems ubiquitous throughout the many departments and geographies of almost every organization, IT can help provide the consistency needed to effectively systematize governance. Therefore, IT governance, risk, and compliance play an integral role in any GRC initiative.

This chapter focuses on the key roles and responsibilities within the IT Compliance Group in support of GRC and the key guidelines and practices that can help enable a successful IT risk and compliance environment.

IT and GRC—Perfect Together

The management of risk and compliance should generally be done throughout the entire enterprise at all levels. But GRC can be particularly critical for the IT organization because IT is responsible for the systems and applications that support the needs of the business.

Regardless of other GRC initiatives being undertaken by the organization, a lack of governance within IT can threaten to undermine even well-intentioned enterprise governance efforts.

For example, consider an organization with a culture that emphasizes exemplary customer support—a worthwhile goal, to be sure. In such an organization, IT staff members may have to be educated on the need to balance their sense of urgency to support their customers at all costs (for example, through quick system updates) with the need to protect the integrity of their IT environment. While change-control procedures may be time-consuming to follow, they can contribute to good governance.

IT GRC Roles

To understand how IT GRC operates in large organizations, let's look at the typical roles of the IT Compliance Group and the IT Compliance Officer.

A business unit executive owns the business processes that deliver value to the organization. Similarly, IT Compliance Group is usually responsible for ensuring that the company's IT processes, procedures, and systems are in compliance with external regulatory mandates, industry requirements, and internal corporate policies. This team, often working with the Governance, Risk and Compliance (GRC) team described in chapter 6, can advise the business unit executive about IT-related compliance issues, although they stop short of setting policy.

You need to know some terminology used in this chapter in order to follow this discussion. A *policy* is a high-level statement of what the corporation wants to achieve. A *business process* is a broad collection of activities performed in support of a *policy*. A *procedure* is a series of discrete steps or activities that takes inputs and produces specific outputs. A *process* consists of a collection of related business or IT *procedures*.

The typical IT Compliance Group understands IT risk and, because it's independent, can be an objective observer of the IT business processes. It typically maintains independence from the responsibility for operating controls, so it can act as an objective testing body to be leveraged by other departments, such as internal audit, to provide an understanding of how well IT controls are operating. For example, Sarbanes-Oxley (SOX) auditors may rely on the IT Compliance Group to test all of the SOX IT controls.

Generally, an IT Compliance Group has no controlling ownership responsibilities over day-to-day business processes. However, it can measure the processes and say objectively that IT is operating within the risk tolerance of the enterprise as defined by the executive leadership team, or it can report deviations. In this regard, the IT Compliance Group can provide a valuable feedback mechanism that helps the business unit executive understand whether the right decisions are being made.

A company's IT Compliance Officer is an independent person who monitors compliance, measures risks, and reports related findings to the organization. He or she often reports to the Chief Information Officer (CIO) and may have a dotted-line relationship to the Chief Compliance Officer (CCO), as shown in Figure 7-1. The IT Compliance Officer is responsible for helping executive leadership understand how IT's decisions affect the organization's compliance posture and risk-tolerance levels.

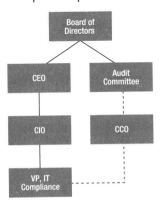

Figure 7-1. Potential reporting structure of IT Compliance

The IT Compliance Officer reviews policies to identify gaps and advises the company on modifying existing policies or creating new policies to fill those gaps. In addition, he or she advises IT on designing processes that carry out policy. The IT Compliance Group then performs testing to ensure adherence with the policies.

Operational line managers are usually responsible for individual procedures that make up a business process. The IT Compliance Officer reviews these procedures to see whether they comply with policies and whether they contain controls to mitigate risk.

The Challenge of Risk vs. Cost

In evaluating and reporting on IT risk, you must often make important trade-offs. This is particularly true in the area of cost. In some cases, risk reduction beyond a defined level of risk isn't worth the cost of mitigation. Let's look at a hypothetical example to understand this common tradeoff.

Consider the increased security risk introduced when employees who need to access sensitive data change from working within a corporate office to working remotely (from home, for instance). Within an office, employees may need to swipe a badge to access that office, and then enter a password to access sensitive data—providing "dual authentication." Remote employees would not be swiping badges to enter an office, therefore decreasing security, perhaps to intolerable levels depending on the nature of the business and the data. Employing smart card protection, the equivalent of swiping a badge for remote employees, could re-establish "dual authentication," though perhaps at great expense as each remote employee would require a smart card and a card reader. A less expensive alternative, which may fall within acceptable risk tolerances, could be issuing smart cards and card readers to only those employees who had a business need to access sensitive data.

In another example of the need to weigh risk versus cost, consider security over a wireless network. Implementing monitoring devices that let you know if any rogue wireless access points have been added to your network is an expensive proposition. If doing so takes you beyond the limits of your anticipated budget, the IT Compliance Group may want to have an objective discussion with the CIO about the risk exposure created by the wireless infrastructure investment.

IT Compliance Controls

An *IT compliance control* is a procedure, a technology, or both, that is intended to help ensure the correct operation of a set of IT processes related to compliance. Although this chapter doesn't provide details about specific controls you should use to achieve successful IT compliance, you may want to consider some of the areas set forth below:

- *Identity and access management*: Management of all user identities and accounts, and control of their access to critical IT resources.

- *Vulnerability management*: Controls to ensure that the current versions of software packages are being used on relevant systems, so that system and network vulnerabilities are both known and minimized.

- *Threat management*: Controls used to detect, prevent, and reduce the impact of various types of malware, including viruses, spam, rootkits, and attacks of all kinds.

- *Information management*: Controls that prevent unauthorized access to critical information such as corporate electronic records, and that enable e-discovery of email and records.

- *Segregation of duties*: Controls used to prevent an individual from having combinations of privileges that would allow improper actions to take place.

- *Change and configuration management*: Controls to ensure that all changes to system configurations are effectively tracked and managed, and that the configurations are always current and well documented.

- *IT Project Life Cycle (also called Software Development Life Cycle [SDLC])*: Controls to ensure that software implementations meet business requirements and have the highest probability of being implemented on time, on budget, and with high quality.

- *Operations management*: Management to ensure that IT operations are running effectively. Controls around job scheduling and backup/recovery occur in this area.

- *Disaster recovery*: Controls to ensure continuity so that, in the event of a disaster, critical IT services are available.

IT GRC Principles

When you're designing an infrastructure or set of procedures to support and monitor IT compliance activities, you may want to keep a few principles in mind. Let's look at some of these principles.

Use Best Practices

A compliance audit can be a painful and expensive process. The definition of what constitutes *adequate controls* for a given regulation can be very subjective. This complicates compliance audits because they often involve discussions with auditors relating to the effectiveness of an organization's controls. Still, we encourage people to think of audits in a positive light, in that they help ensure that you're adequately managing risks.

One way to attempt to simplify these audits, as well as help ensure effective controls, is to follow an industry-recognized best practice. These specifications are usually the result of much work by a large group of recognized experts. You may want to use standards and best practices to challenge where you are today. By looking at the delta between your current processes, procedures, and controls and those of the standard(s) you selected, you can engage in an objective conversation about what you want to achieve.

A number of common best practices are in wide adoption. The Control Objectives for IT (COBIT) is produced by the Information Systems Audit and Control Association (ISACA) and is one of the most widely adopted standards for IT controls. IT standards are also available from the National Institute of Standards and Technology (NIST), a federal technology agency that develops and promotes measurement, standards, and technology. Other common frameworks have been issued by the International

Organization of Standards (ISO) and include the following, which may be of particular interest to IT organizations with multinational interests:

- *ISO 20000*: Delivery and management of IT services (closely related to ITIL®)[1]

- *ISO 27000*: Best practices for IT security

- *ISO 38500*: A control framework for IT governance[2]

You should select standards and best practices to follow depending on what you're trying to achieve.

You can use standards to simplify and improve your IT compliance processes. Let's look at an example where an organization is trying to achieve ISO 20000 certification. The purpose of this certification is to ensure that the organization is operating according to the requirements of ITIL. Line managers may believe their processes to be compliant, but without an independent certification, the claims may not be easily validated. Prior to the actual certification review, the IT Compliance organization may want to take line managers through a pre-assessment phase that evaluates the procedures to see if they meet the requirements of ITIL (ISO 20000). If it's determined that a given procedure doesn't precisely meet the goals of the standard, the procedure may need to be changed, and the company may need to revise its overarching policy as well. But this evaluation can result in a simplification of the IT process, which in turn can lead to reduced costs to manage and test it.

---

[1] ITIL® is a registered trademark, and a registered community trademark of the Office of Government Commerce, and is registered in the U.S. Patent and Trademark Office.

[2] International Standards Organization (ISO), ISO/IEC 20000 Information Technology–Service Management, ISO/IEC 27000 Information technology–Security techniques–Information security management systems–Overview and vocabulary, ISO/IEC 38500 Corporate governance of information technology, http://www.iso.org (accessed 1 December 2009).

In the final step of ISO 20000 certification, the organization has external auditors come in and review its service-delivery processes to ensure they're compliant with the ISO 20000 standard. With this certification in hand, the organization can be more confident that its processes are well-designed and effective. This is important because it helps mitigate risk and gives reasonable assurance that the company's processes are consistently delivering the efficiency gains for which they're designed.

Proactive Control Design

In addition to *regulatory controls,* you may want to consider defining *operational controls* based on best practices or standard frameworks. Strong operational controls can help demonstrate compliance with certain regulations. A strong control environment can also help reap potential benefits when new regulations are introduced. The speed with which you may be able to address new regulations by mapping their requirements to the existing control environment may help provide a competitive edge over organizations subject to the same regulations.

Because many regulations have an element of security (for example, SOX, PCI, HIPAA, the Gramm-Leach-Bliley Act), focusing on security controls may be productive. Security controls for some regulations may overlap. Therefore, identifying redundant controls through controls rationalization, which is described in detail later in this chapter, may yield potential benefits.

Determine the Maturity of Your Controls

Before you undertake a partial or complete redesign of your controls, you may want to determine the maturity level of your current controls. Less mature controls tend to be more expensive and are generally more prone to failure than controls at a higher level of maturity.

One technique that's used by some organizations is Capability Maturity Model Integration (CMMI). This approach provides organizations with elements for effective process improvement. The CMMI model defines levels of process maturity and has gained a high level of acceptance in many large organizations today.[3]

Maturity Level 1 - *Initial*

At this level processes are typically undocumented and in a state of dynamic change, tending to be driven in an *ad hoc*, uncontrolled and reactive manner by users or events.

Maturity Level 2 - *Managed*

At this level, processes are planned and repeatable.

Maturity Level 3 - *Defined*

At this level, there are sets of defined and documented standard processes established and subject to some degree of improvement over time.

Maturity Level 4 – *Quantitatively Managed*

At this level, processes are managed using quality and performance metrics.

Maturity Level 5 - *Optimizing*

At this level, the focus is on continually improving process performance.[4]

By categorizing all controls according to their relative maturity, it becomes easier to determine where you should focus remediation activity, such as controls redesign.

---

[3] Carnegie Mellon Software Engineering Institute, Capability Maturity Model Integration (CMMI), http://www.sei.cmu.edu/cmmi (*see* CMMI models for details) (accessed 1 December 2009).

[4] http://www.sei.cmu.edu/cmmi

Automate Controls

One of the biggest challenges in the design and monitoring of compliance controls relates to automation. Manual controls involve human intervention, decision-making, and often paperwork. Manual controls have three major problems: they're more expensive because they involve human activity, they can be error-prone for the same reason, and they aren't necessarily scalable as the number of transactions increases. For example, consider a simple control requiring a manager to approve access requests by signing a form. This control works well in an environment with 100 employees, but it's likely to be onerous in an environment where the 100 grows to 1,000.

Automation of controls can help reduce these problems. Controls can be monitored, and deviation from policy can often be decreased, or at least detected, through the use of technology. And by automating controls, the burden on your staff doesn't grow proportionately as your environment grows. Automating controls has the potential to allow large populations to be managed as easily as small ones.

This can also be helpful as a company enters new markets or engages in mergers or acquisitions. Sometimes, a large increase in employee population occurs suddenly; and unless IT processes are automated to the extent that allows these new populations to be accommodated quickly, significant IT disruption can occur. In some cases, these disruptions can have very negative impacts on the enterprise.

A challenge for IT governance may be to justify the expense of automated controls through a formal investment request process. If an audit identifies a process subject to a greater risk of manual error, then you may have a good argument for spending money for automation. The issue becomes whether to maintain the manual process (and accept the associated risk), do some level of mitigation, or significantly reduce or eliminate that risk through automation. To make these decisions, some key questions might include: What is our risk tolerance? What are the cost benefits? Can this control be completely or partially automated? How will this impact the achievement of our business goals? Answering these questions will help you to make the best possible decision in each unique circumstance.

Here's an example to further illustrate the benefits of automated controls. An organization can create a role-based security model with automated provisioning (granting) of access based on predefined roles. Suppose all employees who are in the marketing department automatically receive access to a particular marketing application. Automation can be put in place to provision the access any time an employee is added to the marketing department and, conversely, to deprovision the access whenever anyone leaves the department. By automating the provisioning process, you eliminate the need for a manual signature to approve the access request. Access approvals (if required) can be done using automated workflow so that each manager can approve the request using their mouse rather than signing a paper form. When all approvals have been done, access rights are granted on a real-time basis. You have immediately saved your approvers' time as well as reduced the probability of error.

The corresponding automation of the deprovisioning process has similar advantages, but it also helps decrease certain security vulnerabilities. When a disgruntled employee is terminated, his or her access rights and accounts need to be terminated immediately. Even a small delay in removing access may pose an unacceptable risk to the corporation. Automation of the process may be the only viable way to achieve this.

Although this is a simplistic example, it illustrates how an investment in technology can automate compliance controls, thereby saving time and money and making the controls more effective. Each organization is different and should evaluate where such automations are possible and will provide the biggest benefit. The controls that are the best candidates for automation are generally those manual controls that cost the most to operate or are the most prone to failure.

Automated controls can also be important when organizations are faced with the risk-versus-cost tradeoff considered earlier. Controls automation can lead to greater efficiency and therefore lower compliance costs. But automated controls are often also less prone to failures than manual controls (because humans are fallible). So, as manual controls are automated, both overall risk and total costs can potentially be reduced, helping to eliminate the typical tradeoff between these two important requirements. Although investments are required in order to automate controls, the investment return comes with increased efficiency of the operation.

Rationalize Your Controls

As a result of information silos, discussed in Chapter 1, companies may be maintaining overlapping controls. For example, some companies have a set of SOX-specific controls that may overlap or even be redundant with the controls implemented for PCI (Payment Card Industry) compliance. This may result in excessive costs and effort involved in testing, documenting, and auditing these redundant controls.

The solution to minimizing such overlap is to rationalize your controls across multiple regulations and best practices to remove controls that test for the same risk and to better leverage controls for multiple purposes. Because the requirements of one regulation may be similar but not identical to those of another regulation, it may be challenging to implement controls that meet the needs of multiple regulations. The payoff can be significant if this is done successfully, but may require extensive analysis and diligence.

One approach to reduce these challenges is to adopt a regulatory repository of regulations and control definitions. One widely adopted repository is Network Frontier's Unified Compliance Framework (UCF). According to the UCF website,

> *"The UCF harmonizes IT controls from over 400 international regulatory requirements, standards and guidelines into a single set of straightforward requirements that clearly show the many points where global, state and industry regulations overlap, reducing compliance complexity and cutting the costs of regulatory management and audits."* [5]

---

[5] Network Frontier, Unified Compliance Framework (UCF), http://www.unifiedcompliance.com (accessed 10 November 2009).

Rationalization of controls can help provide a reduced and more meaningful set of controls, which can also make it easier to assign accountability for the execution of each control. Each control can be aligned with a person who is responsible for executing it, and that accountability can be helpful when problems with the control arise. In addition, the reduction in the number of controls and the fact that each control tends to meet multiple requirements can increase the sense of responsibility that each control owner has.

As part of the analysis of your controls, both to determine their maturity and to look for areas of overlap, you may want to look at similar controls across the organization. Taking a purely localized approach to controls rationalization is better than doing nothing, but it only reduces the scope of the problem; it doesn't move you toward eliminating it. In addition, you may find controls that either aren't associated with a specific risk or aren't necessary. This can result in further optimization of your controls.

Another reason you may want to rationalize controls is that when multiple controls cover the same task, you might foster a lack of commitment among the employees involved in those related controls. They may feel that "I don't have to perform my check, because someone else will do theirs." Or, "I'm doing this check, but I know Johnny is doing the check behind me; so if I don't catch it, Johnny will." The problem is that Johnny may be saying, "I don't have to do my check because Rob will catch it." If that logic is pervasive, the possibility that no one is checking increases significantly. You need to be sure your controls are meaningful and that everyone supports them and understands their role in executing them.

Organizations, especially those in reactive mode, may be tempted to throw controls at a problem, without taking the time to rationalize them to avoid overlap. To adapt to ongoing businesses changes, continuous improvement is needed. This, in part, comes from regularly rationalizing controls and establishing or verifying clear accountability. When control owners are held responsible for consistently executing their controls, and they understand the purpose of the controls, the happy byproduct is that they may go beyond merely performing tasks without understanding their purpose and may begin looking for improvements and ensuring that controls evolve along with the needs of the business.

One of my favorite examples of the benefits of clear control ownership arises with my kids when I ask them to mitigate the risk of someone slipping in our driveway after a snowstorm. They look and me and say, "Why can't you just say 'shovel the snow' like everybody else's father?" I answer, "Shoveling isn't the control I'm looking for. When you do shovel, you tend to leave about an inch of snow that will eventually turn to ice. I need you to mitigate the risk of someone slipping in the driveway. Shoveling is just one control. Sometimes, depending on the weather conditions, additional controls are needed, such as throwing down salt or sand." At this point, my kids' eyes are glazed over, and they say, "Dad, stop talking like that." Undeterred, I continue, "Depending on how the weather changes, we may be able to rationalize the controls and only do the shoveling." The point is, when they understand the objective, versus just doing a task they're told to do, they'll do a better job because they know what it is they're trying to achieve.

One of my first initiatives at CA was to undertake a controls rationalization project. With operations in 45 countries, we must comply with a broad range of regulations as well as our own internal controls. By using CA GRC Manager, we were able to reduce our number of IT controls from 500 to 250. We've had similar success with reducing the total number of business controls by half.

It's important that the IT Compliance Officer understands and can communicate the overlap in controls occurring with automated controls as opposed to manual controls. Certain regulations and/or policies may require general computing controls. For example, automated security controls required by one regulation may also be required by another. Conversely, a manual control like performing a bank reconciliation is likely to be valid only in a single business process. This nature of IT controls applying to many business applications and processes needs to be clearly articulated when you're determining the business value behind decisions to automate controls. Often, people outside IT don't understand this concept. The point might need to be reinforced to help get buy-in on the value proposition behind automating controls.

Clearly Identify Control Owners

In some large organizations, ownership of certain business processes, including their related controls, isn't clearly defined. This can potentially create problems of responsibility, because it may be unclear who is responsible not only for determining whether the control is operating effectively, but also for correcting any defective controls.

Having control owners self-assess their controls can be a way to increase accountability—and pride of ownership—and may correlate to a higher pass rate for their respective controls. This is because control owners know that they need to assess the effectiveness of the operation of those controls and report back how well the controls are mitigating risks.

A challenge to implementing self-assessments is the subjectivity that comes into play. Reporting on self-assessments should be done within a common framework so that when you compare risks, you're comparing apples to apples. The goal is for assessment results to be as objective as possible. For example, if you ask people to rate the effectiveness of their control from 1–5, some people will look at a 5 as very good and say, "I do everything very well; therefore, I rate my control as a 5." If you use a capability maturity model with clear definitions of each score, you may achieve a more objective rating of the controls.

Define Risk Metrics

As stated earlier, controls can be implemented either to meet the needs of regulatory requirements or to mitigate a defined risk, or both. To more effectively determine the impact of a control on a given risk, you may want to consider establishing guidelines and procedures that help ensure a consistent method for risk assessment across the enterprise. The IT Compliance Group may want to consider working with the Chief Risk Officer or an enterprise-wide risk organization, such as the GRC team described in Chapter 6, to help ensure that it measures IT risk the same way risk is measured throughout the firm. Even though groups may be managing different types of risks, the basic processes and terminology for risk identification, assessment, and measurement should be the same across the enterprise. A proactive and consistent risk approach can be beneficial to the corporation in the long run because it can be better managed operationally, and the business may have better visibility into total corporate risk.

A common set of risk metrics can be helpful to establish a consistent terminology and aid in risk-trending analysis. As risks increase in severity, it's essential that you clearly identify emerging risks so that management can begin mitigation activities quickly. Without an objective method of risk assessment, this trending analysis can be difficult.

Common metrics used in many organizations are Key Risk Indicators (KRIs), which we discussed in Chapter 4. Recall that these are numerical representations of the level of risk in a given area. They can be useful because they're often a leading indicator of changes in other areas of corporate performance. For example, let's say you define a KRI to be the turnover rate of critical IT systems administrators. Anything over 0% can be harmful; but because that is unreasonable, you can define a range of values (say, below 10%) that is tolerable. When the value of that KRI exceeds that threshold, downstream impacts may affect more important financial parameters. To continue the example, if that KRI value is high, it may affect the delivery of key services to your value chain, which ultimately can impact your corporate revenues. Therefore, each environment should consider defining its own KRIs and their acceptable thresholds so you can predict the downstream effect that may occur when a KRI exceeds its threshold.

Risk is based on two factors: *likelihood* and *impact*. The goal of risk management, of course, is to make sure high-impact risks have a very low likelihood of occurrence. Whether you choose to allow low-impact risks to have a high likelihood depends on your specific environment, business objectives, and risk tolerance. But as you develop your risk management strategy, including the metrics you'll use to measure risk, you should always keep the basic relationship between these two concepts in mind. Figure 7-2 illustrates.

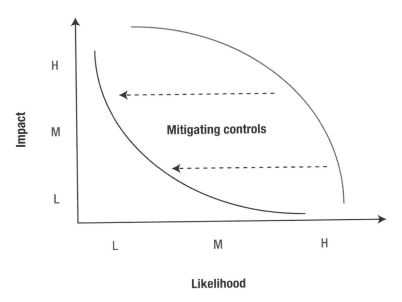

Figure 7-2. Ideal risk management profile

In Figure 7-2, the bottom curved line represents optimal risk tolerance—the amount of risk a company is willing to accept. You can see that high-impact risks have a low likelihood, and high-likelihood risks have low impact. The top line represents inherent risk. This is the amount of risk before any mitigating controls are applied. The space in the middle represents the amount of risk a company's controls must mitigate to reduce the risk to a tolerable level. The residual risk is represented by the bottom line. This is the risk left after mitigating controls have been applied. It's possible for your residual risk to be above your risk tolerance. When this is the case, discussions must take place to determine the best way to address the situation (for example, develop remediation plans, accept the risk, etc.).

These metrics are very important because they enable you to measure and do trending analysis on the effectiveness of your controls. For example, dashboards can show you the areas where controls are the weakest (that is, where your residual risk is greater than your risk tolerance) so that you can identify areas for controls redesign.

IT organizations should consider having defined risk tolerances that are based on metrics. Some organizations work by the seat of their pants and don't necessarily understand risks from a formal perspective. They may have a sense that everything is fine, but what they're really saying is, "I *think* all my risks are in alignment, but I don't know for sure."

For example, a major discount retailer that likely thought its security was good enough wound up having its network penetrated and customers' credit card data sold on the open market. This created a slew of regulatory issues for the company as well as bad customer relations and bad publicity.

Communicating the Compliance Message

Many times, compliance managers attempt to communicate the status of compliance or risk to executives in the business but fail to adequately convey the impact. This is often because the communication is done at a level that doesn't resonate with the business owner. Business owners may not "speak IT," so risks must be communicated in a language they understand. Using a risk framework adopted across the enterprise can help facilitate a meaningful dialogue between the IT Compliance Officer and the business line managers.

When delivering the compliance message, IT Compliance Officers may want to consider positioning the message not necessarily as a recommendation to implement a technology, but rather as a means to reduce a risk. The message should relate the risk that has been identified—whether it's a design flaw, a gap, or an ineffective control—with how it impacts the operation. In addition, this risk analysis should not only describe the current status, but also help the business manager understand the impact of this risk on their business. You want to say, "This is the gap we identified. This is how it impacts the operation. Therefore, the risk is…." The risk should answer the fundamental question, "So what?"

An example will help make the point. Let's say that IT would like to institute strong encryption technology for the transmission of credit card transaction data. IT shouldn't say, "We need to install 128-bit encryption on our servers." The business owners may not understand what that means or what the benefits are. Instead, IT should communicate the risk: "If we don't have sufficient encryption, we may leave ourselves vulnerable to having our data compromised and having it used for fraudulent purposes." That is something the business owners can understand. The risk always exists that the credit card information can be stolen, but the business needs to get to a *reasonable* level of assurance that is within the level of risk tolerance the organization has adopted. Some business managers may view this as a purely IT issue that doesn't affect them at all. Yet theft of customer credit card information can have dramatic and sometimes catastrophic impacts on the business, in terms of governmental fines, loss of customers, reputational damage, and compensation costs. All of these factors can dramatically affect the business, so the introduction of stronger encryption needs to be positioned in such a way as to highlight its role in the reduction of this risk.

In addition to communication with business owners, communication with other departments is critical for effective corporate governance. The people who are integrating governance efforts should meet frequently. These may include the IT Compliance Group, the SOX group, internal auditors, the GRC team, legal counsel, external auditors, the Chief Risk Officer, and others. The goal is to ensure that integration efforts are well-planned and successful—and that good governance is employed while working toward good governance across the enterprise.

Conclusion

Of the areas within corporate governance, IT GRC is among the most challenging and important. The IT infrastructure is generally a key element of critical business processes, and any failure in that infrastructure can have a significant impact on corporate activity. Therefore, IT governance must be tied in with all other governance initiatives. Its role will continue to increase as more processes and controls become technology-enabled.

IT is a major component in the unified, consistent approach to compliance. As new regulations come out, if you have automated controls already in place, compliance may be facilitated by mapping regulations to existing controls. Increased agility and reduced compliance costs can serve as a competitive advantage. While your competitors are struggling with the effort and costs required to support new regulations, you can adapt quickly and spend your money on strategic business initiatives.

Systematizing governance is a worthwhile undertaking for organizations looking to take advantage of the efficiencies that come with repeatable processes and automated controls. But systematizing governance is far from a set-and-forget endeavor. It requires continued diligence, clear responsibilities, and an organizational commitment to keep good governance top-of-mind. An effective IT Compliance Group provides not only the IT muscle needed for the systematizing, but also the GRC expertise to advise business owners on the existence of risks, on recommendations to mitigate those risks, and on establishing processes and controls that increasingly raise the governance standard within the organization.

Governance and Portfolio Management

by John Meyer and Helge Scheil

We've said previously that governance is essentially the creation and management of the culture, the policies, procedures, and controls that help ensure a company will meet its business goals. Good governance requires active stewardship of all of an organization's investments. This stewardship is led by senior executives but is often managed further down in the organization. Project management techniques have traditionally been used to track these investments, and most companies have become skilled at managing and measuring project costs and schedules. However, Project and Portfolio Management (PPM) brings an additional level of sophistication to project management by tracking investments across portfolios of projects.

Why manage clusters of projects (a portfolio) rather than treat each individually? PPM delivers an extensive, prioritized view of initiatives the organization has considered, planned, and undertaken. Portfolio management furthermore provides visibility into each initiative's performance, schedule, cost structure, risk score, and business value. Every resource commitment is regarded as a *business* investment and is scrutinized just as financial investments would be scrutinized—especially during tough economic times. (See "The Importance of Governance in a Changing Economy") in this chapter.

THE IMPORTANCE OF GOVERNANCE IN A CHANGING ECONOMY

by Steve Romero, IT Governance Evangelist, CA, Inc.

Excerpt from "Commit to Good Governance—In Sickness and in Health," The IT Governance Evangelist Blog, 15 December 2008, community.ca.com/blogs/theitgovernanceevangelist/archive/2008/12.aspx

Companies continue to deal with the ramifications of the current economic downturn and the resulting consequences. Everyone is. In times like these, it's critical to remember that good governance is more important than ever. Fortunately, there are people who get this.

As I write this post, I am on a plane to Atlanta to present on the purpose and promise of Project and Portfolio Management. The attendance for this presentation has increased in recent days. Instead of people canceling their plans to attend, more have committed to an evening discussing this critical business process.

I am assuming the increase is due to the recognition that good Project and Portfolio Management is even more critical during tough times. We can afford to make mistakes in regard to our Enterprise investments when we have plenty of money. But when belts get tightened, we better make sure we are getting optimal value out of those few initiatives we can afford to undertake.

Organizations with good governance already have the conventions in place to make the appropriate changes in strategy, plans, and operations to respond to current circumstances. Firms with sound PPM processes need simply decrease financial allocation to this portfolio, increase investment in that portfolio, adjust the risk quotient to another portfolio, etc. These adjustments are made in response to the changes in strategic direction necessary to keep the company afloat, if not profitable, in these turbulent times.

Organizations without good governance are now incented to correct this deficiency. They find they can no longer afford to make poor decisions. Their portfolios of investments need to be reasoned and rationale, so their decisions better not be arbitrary or ill-informed. Now, more than ever, good governance will help ensure decisions are fact-based, well-founded, realized, and subsequently measured to determine if they were the right decisions.

Times are difficult for all of us. One of the few silver-linings for me will be the advent of governance improvements that will inevitably take place. It is my fervent wish that these governance processes, conventions, and mechanisms will continue to be advocated and fostered—even after this latest economic storm has passed. My hope is that enterprises will come to realize the essential nature of good governance, in good times as well as bad. Only then will they be ready for the next storm that comes.

Historically, the discipline of portfolio management was first adopted by IT organizations as a defensive strategy against the surge in demand for IT resources. IT portfolio management is the discipline of creating and managing a mix of IT investments (projects, applications, and assets) to help diminish risk and increase value using a finite pool of IT resources. As IT's contribution toward delivering successful projects and services to the business grew, so too did the need for greater PPM adoption. The Project Management Office (PMO) soon began to emerge to help identify and govern PPM best practices. Meanwhile, software solutions were implemented to automate and scale the processes adopted. Over the last several years, as organizations worked to quantify the value of PPM in IT, these same practices began to seep into other parts of the organization, including research and development (to support the product development life cycle), marketing and advertising (to support campaign management), and cross-functional areas including mergers and acquisitions and enterprise portfolio management, to name a few.

Just as IT portfolio management is a subset of corporate portfolio management, IT governance is a subset of corporate governance. The goal of governance is to engage all relevant stakeholders to establish decisions, rights, and controls for achieving a desirable outcome. Portfolio management then helps to create and manage the mix of investments, diminish risk, and increase value using a finite pool of resources. Both disciplines are related, and the commonality is what makes a systematized approach more effective.

Portfolio management should first be conducted at the corporate or enterprise level. Senior leaders set the corporate strategy for the organization. Based on the established long-term strategy, business leaders then construct the fiscal strategy to align with the corporate goals and budget allocation. Included in the fiscal year portfolio are a variety of initiatives that may include mergers and acquisitions, geographic expansions, product development advances, facilities planning, IT systems upgrades, and so on. The intent is to define an optimal mix of initiatives, supported by a finite group of people and funding, to best achieve an organization's goals. After it's defined and prioritized, the portfolio is given to executive management for review and approval. When the portfolio is approved, it must be quantified, continually assessed, and executed to help ensure that business goals are being met throughout the portfolio's life cycle.

Understand that when we discuss the portfolio here, it doesn't refer to a single portfolio of investments. Rather, in most organizations, the overall portfolio comprises multiple portfolios that are aggregated together to achieve an overarching goal.

Sounds simple enough, but undefined processes, disparate management tools, manual reporting systems, and a lack of cross-functional collaboration can make portfolio management a resource-intensive and challenging task for many IT organizations. However, by implementing a structured, repeatable PPM discipline (which is often supported by industry best practices, defined processes, and software solutions), organizations are better able to effectively govern their portfolio of investments.

Bringing It All Together

It can be difficult to achieve effective governance without an accurate view of the collective needs of all the business units that rely on IT to support their strategic goals.

Many IT organizations are in reactive mode when it comes to supporting business needs (commonly referred to as *demand*). This demand takes on multiple forms and includes strategic/transformational projects (projects with significant impact on the business, such as creating a website for online sales); tactical projects to help run the business; and even casual, one-off operational service requests, which may include moves, changes, problems, and fixes. By adhering to a rigorous portfolio management process, you can capture this demand in a central location, evaluate it across multiple criteria, and execute if the request is approved. However, don't underestimate the importance of demand management. It can be a big obstacle to portfolio management but can also be most rewarding, helping to ensure that resources are allocated to the highest-value priorities.

You may want to establish a formal process to manage strategic requests. The process should engage stakeholders and consider the following:

- A solid business case

- A spending plan

- A benefits plan, with stated, achievable, and measurable benefits

- Effective scoring of each investment metric (risk, cost, alignment, effort, and so on)

For operational or *lights on* requests (those requests that are necessary to keep the corporate engine running), resources are generally allocated immediately, and the work is tracked from beginning through completion. Although these requests affect resource availability, they don't require the same analysis that's necessary to plan for managing large-scale strategic projects over an extended period of time. But don't underestimate, as many organizations do, the impact these "keep the lights on" activities have on your resource pool. In fact, these tactical, operational requests can account for a majority of the work being completed by an IT organization. For strategic projects, as suggested earlier, you need a more formal, apples-to-apples comparison to make informed, accurate trade-off decisions to determine the appropriate investment mix within a portfolio.

Comparing Apples to Apples

In organizations that aren't practicing portfolio governance, initiatives may be selected based on corporate politics or cost alone. Pet projects of determined proponents may be awarded funding while more strategic projects go begging. What's needed instead is the ability to make objective apples-to-apples comparisons to improve the quality of investment decisions. Analytical tools can help you perform what-if analyses to evaluate, compare, and select better investment scenarios. What's more, PPM as a discipline helps enable organizations to establish key performance metrics connected to business outcomes and enterprise objectives, to further support comparisons between projects.

Let's examine Figure 8-1. Each bubble represents an initiative that can be compared in an apples-to-apples fashion to other initiatives in terms of key metrics around risks, planned cost, and priority. What observations can be made? What decisions can you come to?

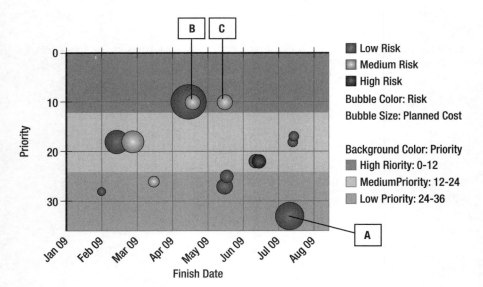

Figure 8-1. Portfolio planning and analysis gives you insight into investment cost, priority, schedule, and risk, as depicted in this CA Clarity PPM screenshot

First, by looking at the background shading and placement, you can see the initiatives ranked by priority—the lower the number on the vertical scale, the greater the priority. In this figure, the size of the bubble indicates the level of cost, and the shading of the bubble indicates the level of risk. You can easily determine that bubble A is the lowest-priority initiative. Although it's low risk (as depicted by the interior shading), the size of the bubble indicates that it's the second most expensive planned initiative. With this information in hand, you may decide to reinvest these funds elsewhere.

Next, by looking at bubbles B and C in the top third of the chart, you can see that they're high priorities, but they have a medium level of risk (as depicted by the shade of the bubble) associated with them. You could evaluate each of these initiatives further to determine if additional funding and resources taken from the low-priority initiative (bubble A) could help lower the risk associated with these two higher-priority initiatives. If so, this is an excellent example of how to optimally and intelligently allocate resources to support high-value initiatives.

Having a clear investment model allows you to focus resources on what is important. It also has an unseen effect. When customers understand the investment criteria (what is being funded, and what isn't) they are discouraged from making requests for projects that will most likely be rejected. This can help lower the incoming demand on your organization.

Optimizing Your Most Valuable Asset

As your organization makes investment decisions, you should not only evaluate cost, risk, priority, and demand; you should also leverage your human resources to deliver successful projects. Not including resource management and utilization in the overall process can have a detrimental effect on portfolio performance and ultimately the satisfaction of key stakeholders in the business.

Managing resources shouldn't be accomplished by merely assigning open resources to open projects. Instead, to best utilize resources organizations, you may want to consider the following:

- *Balance resource capacity and project demand*: Give resource managers the tools they need to identify, locate, and deploy qualified internal or external staff to meet business demand.

- *Reassess the current portfolio*: Realize that certain adjustments need to be continually made in your current portfolio(s) to meet changing organizational goals. Conducting a what-if analysis will help you identify how and where to shift resources.

- *Don't lose sight of the future*: Managing resources can be a daunting task if managed on a daily basis. The value of comprehensive resource management is the ability to not only manage capacity but also plan for future resource requirements. By effectively tracking, categorizing, and organizing resource skills, you can proactively identify gaps and redundancies to improve future resource planning.

Doing Things Right: Managing Performance and Risk

The portfolio management part of PPM is about establishing criteria and processes for doing the right things; the project management component is about doing those things right. This powerful combination helps ensure your organization is working on the highest-value initiatives and delivering them with consistency and predictability. Without this rigor and discipline in place, organizations often become inefficient and underproductive.

To achieve the optimum portfolio, performance should be continually managed, both from a project and a portfolio perspective. However, manually micromanaging the status of each project can be inefficient. Managing performance by exception can be much more effective. In this case, you review each portfolio and drill down only into areas that indicate a performance disparity.

As you look to further ensure predictability across your portfolio, you must work to proactively mitigate risk. It's important to accept that you'll never truly eliminate risk; rather, you should try to keep risk at a level that both your executive team and auditors find acceptable.

To mitigate risk, what Key Performance Indicators (KPIs) do you need to effectively manage? Time and money are most commonly monitored and generally, most organizations have a good grasp on this today. For some organizations, competitive and regulatory changes can have profound implications that create new and urgent requirements. PPM makes it easier to manage in an environment that is constantly changing and requires course corrections. To drive consistency and predictability, client satisfaction should also be proactively managed. Project managers must collaborate with business unit leaders, keeping them involved and engaged throughout the project life cycle to help ensure that business requirements are satisfied. Without a continuous feedback loop, projects delivered are at risk of not satisfying business expectations.

Continually assessing performance and mitigating project and portfolio risk helps to drive increased productivity and efficiency, while allowing organizations to quickly adapt to dynamic business conditions. Ultimately, it helps to strengthen the ability to deliver on commitments to the business. Refer to "Case Study: International Beverage Company" in this chapter to see how one company benefited from PPM.

CASE STUDY: INTERNATIONAL BEVERAGE COMPANY

A beverage company was looking to invest in growing markets and innovation in an effort to respond to a declining market demand for their core product. To sustain their market-leading position, they were looking at ways to reduce operational overhead and break into new business areas. This strategy resulted in the acquisition of a number of companies and the development of new, innovative business models. It also had a dramatic impact on the organization's day-to-day operations and the company's IT infrastructure.

During the course of a year, this organization's IT team oversaw around eight large-scale projects plus upward of 150 other smaller IT projects. Coping with the complexity of this IT portfolio, however, became increasingly difficult. It was hard for them to understand how IT projects linked to overall business objectives and how to best prioritize their activities, because IT functions were being managed via hundreds of different spreadsheets, making it impossible to see a single view of the company's IT projects. Each project also had its own separate folder with information about different areas, such as risk management and resource allocation. To view this information across all projects would have required a huge amount of manual effort, so they didn't attempt to gather portfolio-level metrics. With no central view of internal resourcing capabilities, it made it difficult to judge if they could deliver the projects expected by the business.

To overcome these problems, the company decided to implement a project and portfolio management discipline and automated solution, to improve their governance and control. The goal of implementing PPM was to gain:

1. A high-level view of all projects and how they linked to their business objectives

2. The ability to manage IT resources more effectively

3. Improved financial management capabilities

Initially, Project and Portfolio Management proved particularly useful for their annual planning exercise, which now takes two days rather than three to four weeks to complete. They were able to effectively evaluate what resources were needed to support each project and the level of spending and change required by the business. They could also match resources to planned business projects and calculate a more precise annual budget, while identifying projects that couldn't be completed in the next financial year due to resource constraints.

Now, they have committed to using PPM across their global IT operations and are looking to expand to other areas including manufacturing, HR, and new product development.

Communicating Customer Value

Aligning your portfolio of investments to corporate priorities is irrelevant if the end result isn't increased customer value or improved customer satisfaction. After all, an objective of governance is to improve outcomes while avoiding undesirable circumstances.

In many organizations, however, delivering value isn't the toughest challenge. The increase of globalization and outsourcing has created more complex challenges around *communicating* value delivered. Whether it's an improvement in service quality, customer experience, or hard dollar savings, customer value must be communicated to relevant stakeholders across the enterprise. You can help achieve this by first communicating incremental wins to stakeholders. This is intended to help reinforce the value of your PPM processes and demonstrate how everyone's efforts can positively impact the business. As the size and frequency of successful projects increases, organizational culture may also begin to adopt and change to the new paradigm. Stakeholders will become more engaged and more accountable in the process.

Reaping the ROI of PPM

The benefits of portfolio governance are many. It empowers organizations to manage their demand (requests), select the appropriate initiatives, oversee execution, automate controls and their performance metrics, and help ensure that their objectives are realized. This cannot be achieved through project management alone. Together, the project management and portfolio management disciplines help enable you to effectively govern your organization by:

- Collecting all initiatives in a central repository

- Giving you transparency into initiative metrics, including cost, risk, performance, and value

- Allowing you to actively assess and readjust initiatives

- Identifying areas to reallocate your resources to higher-value initiatives

- Empowering you to quantify and communicate value delivered

Although the benefits of PPM can be great (see Figure 8-2), organizations still need to understand the financial benefits, or ROI, to justify their investment in PPM. In an IDC White Paper sponsored by CA, which interviewed over a dozen organizations that implemented PPM, IDC quantified the benefits organizations can achieve when they effectively govern their portfolio of investments.[1] They are as follows:

Cost reduction

- IT project optimization from better project planning and management.
  $49,000 per 100 users annually (59% of total benefits)

- IT operations cost reduction from resources consolidation and IT staff productivity improvement.
  $18,600 per 100 users annually (22% of total benefits)

Revenue increase

- Revenue increase from delivering revenue-generating business applications to market faster.
  $15,200 per 100 users annually (18% of total benefits)

Increased user productivity

- User productivity increase through reducing help-desk issues associated with initial project deployment (first 30 days).
  $700 per 100 users annually (1% of total benefits)[2]

---

[1] IDC Research, "How Project & Portfolio Management Solutions Are Delivering Value to Organizations," White Paper, September 2008.

[2] IDC Research, "How Project & Portfolio Management Solutions Are Delivering Value to Organizations," White Paper, September 2008.

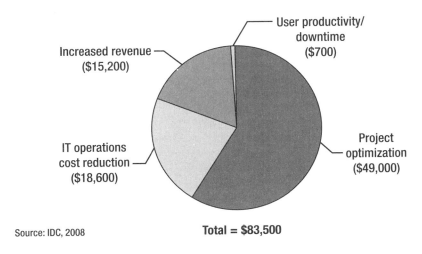

Source: IDC, 2008   **Total = $83,500**

Figure 8-2. Benefits of PPM per 100 employees[3]

Getting Started with Best Practice Frameworks and Methodologies

The question remains: Where do you get started? We don't recommend beginning on your own. Thousands of companies have implemented PPM to support their enterprise governance practices. It only makes sense to take advantage of their triumphs and pitfalls. You can leverage recognized industry frameworks/standards and best-practice methodologies as a good starting point into portfolio management. Some PPM software solutions incorporate these best practices, which include prebuilt report templates, workflows, and portlets to help ease of use and help ensure that the desired business outcome is achieved.

Stage-Gate® is an example of a methodology that is recognized for new product development.

---

[3] IDC Research, "How Project & Portfolio Management Solutions Are Delivering Value to Organizations," White Paper, September 2008.

"The Stage-Gate process is a conceptual and operational road map for moving a new-product project from idea to launch. It has empowered almost 80% of all North American companies to achieve improved returns on their product development dollars." [4]

The Project Management Body of Knowledge[5] (PMBOK®) is another framework used across many enterprises, primarily in IT, in an attempt to document and standardize generally accepted project management information and practices. It's a leading framework that contains fundamental baseline practices to help drive business results in organizations. PMBOK identifies nine areas where processes need to be established to help ensure effective program management.

The Val IT™ framework is another example of an IT framework that has recently emerged. Although not yet widely adopted, Val IT (which complements COBIT®[6]) integrates a set of practical and proven governance principles, processes, practices, and supporting guidelines that helps Boards, executive management, and other enterprise leaders optimize the realization of value from IT investments.[7]

---

[4] Innovation Leader Stage-Gate Inc. Endorses CA Clarity for Managing New Product Development," Press Release, 29 October 2007, http://www.ca.com/us/press/release.aspx?cid=158776 (accessed 1 December 2009).

[5] Project Management Institute, Project Management Body of Knowledge (PMBOK), http://www.pmi.org/Resources/Pages/Library-of-PMI-Global-Standards-Projects.aspx (accessed 1 December 2009).

[6] Information Systems Audit and Control Association (ISACA), Control Objectives for Information and Related Technology (COBIT), http://www.isaca.org/cobit (accessed 1 December 2009).

[7] Information Systems Audit and Control Association (ISACA), Val IT, http://www.isaca.org/valit (accessed 1 December 2009).

Initiated by the U.K. Office of Government Commerce, PRINCE2®[8, 9] is a generic project management method that's widely applied by IT organizations but has also been used worldwide for its scalability and flexibility. Specifically, the PRINCE2 methodology is a framework of processes that uses a set of common components to reduce risk and avoid failure. To achieve this, three techniques are employed: product-based planning, quality review, and change control.

Conclusion

Without PPM, it's difficult for a company to know which initiatives are best aligned with its business strategies and make the most effective use of limited resources. With project management practices alone, if a project comes in on time and within budget, and with the expected features, it may be judged as a success even if it results in minimal cost savings and revenue contribution, or even subpar alignment with corporate objectives.

In contrast, adopting PPM as a corporate discipline provides the foundation necessary for companies to move toward global portfolio governance. By ensuring that projects are chosen for execution in alignment with corporate objectives—and that once chosen, those projects optimally leverage valuable company resources and deliver the expected business results—companies can help ensure that their governance efforts are aligned for success.

---

[8] PRINCE2 is a Registered Trade Mark of the Office of Government Commerce in the United Kingdom and other countries.

[9] Office of Government Commerce, PRINCE2, http://www.prince-officialsite.com.

The Regulatory Environment

by Marc Camm and Christopher Fox

> *"The financial crisis…is not just the result of a missing regulator, a gaping structural gap in the regulatory framework. Rather, it is rooted in the refusal of regulators, lawmakers and executive-branch officials to heed warnings about risks in the system and to use their powers to head them off."* [1]

The pendulum of regulation is swinging in a different direction as a result of the financial crisis that emerged during 2008. You should be prepared not only for a number of new regulations seeking to fill perceived gaps in current regulations, but also for stricter enforcement of existing regulations and demand for more transparency and timely reporting to enable

---

[1] "It's the Regulations, Not the Regulator," *New York Times*, 18 March 2009, http://www.nytimes.com/2009/03/19/opinion/19thu1.html (accessed 1 December 2009).

regulators to manage systemic risk. Regulatory changes are also likely due to these trends:

- Increasingly formalized roles and responsibilities of company Directors.

- Increasing requirements for establishing a formal risk management process.

- Increased transparency of risk management and management decision-making.

- Regulation of rating agencies. Although this may initially focus on credit risk, other types of risk assessment may be required. This change may be international in nature, with Europe taking the lead on regulatory changes.

If regulatory change and compliance with those changes aren't managed properly, organizations may be quickly overwhelmed by complexity and inherent redundancies. Resources may be diverted to address regulation challenges and away from other pressing business objectives. Worse, an organization's reputation and/or profitability may suffer if noncompliance creates reputational damage.

This chapter focuses on some key issues related to the shifting regulatory environment.

The Shifting Regulatory Landscape

Recent experience has demonstrated that one of the fastest ways for an industry to become subject to more regulation is to not comply with existing regulations—or to make the authoritative agency (and some lawmakers) look bad through a widespread or much-publicized failure. Does this mean more regulations will be coming out of the 2008 financial collapse? In a word, "yes." What remains to be seen is how much, how detailed, and how long it will take.

You only need to go back a few years to see how another much publicized and widespread collapse—the worst blackout in the history of North America—altered the compliance playing field (see "Case: The 2003 Blackout").

CASE: THE 2003 BLACKOUT

August 14, 2003, at 4:10 P.M., a massive power fluctuation triggered a cascading blackout that spread within minutes to the northeastern United States and Canada. This huge power failure pulled the plug on some 50 million people in North America and resulted in financial losses of approximately $6 billion. After the lights came back on, regulatory changes—changes that had been considered since the 1965 blackout, but had evolved into industry-driven policies and guidelines without the force of law—became mandated within two years.

As a result of the 2003 blackout and subsequent legislation, the North American Electric Reliability Corporation (NERC), which was established as an industry council in the 1960s and later a nonprofit corporation to facilitate the coordination of U.S. and Canadian power grids, is now the de facto enforcement arm of the U.S. Federal Energy Regulatory Commission (FERC),[2] with the power to enforce through citations and fines.

Today, NERC's standards are mandatory and enforced throughout the United States and several provinces in Canada by NERC's regional sub-organizations. U.S. power-supply companies that violate standards face fines of up to $1 million per day. That's per violation, and penalties can be assessed retroactively. When you're facing a fine that severe, regulatory compliance is serious business.

---

[2] In July 2006, FERC certified NERC as the "electric reliability organization" for the United States, and NERC signed memoranda of understanding with Ontario, Quebec, Nova Scotia, and the National Energy Board of Canada. Source: NERC website, http://www.nerc.com/page.php?cid=1|7|11 (accessed 1 December 2009).

In 2003, would compliance with what had previously been guidelines have prevented the blackout? Perhaps. But we do know a failure occurred, and more regulation and more severe penalties for noncompliance resulted.

Those are the surface issues. The underlying issues are: more complexity involved in staying compliant, greater costs to stay compliant, and greater costs in terms of both reputation and financial impact. For example, a power operator running 80 power plants throughout the United States now needs to comply with NERC regulations across eight regions and deal with eight separate organizations, all with subtle differences and all with the power of mandate. The effective number of regulations reaches into the thousands. In addition to NERC, this power operator also must comply with other mandates, including those of FERC and SOX. Many organizations that operate in a highly regulated environment are in a similar situation.

In the current environment, failures of compliance (whether the fault of individuals, companies, regulatory bodies, or lawmakers) are likely to create more compliance requirements and thus further compound complexity and cost.

Navigating the U.S. Regulatory Environment

The U.S. regulatory environment is best described as the coexistence of multiple regulatory frameworks. The objective of the U.S. regulatory framework is to achieve public policy objectives, such as the orderly operation of financial markets. For example, SOX seeks to prevent future Enrons. Regulations and regulatory agencies are frequently created in reaction to a crisis or highly publicized localized failing that points to potential future failings. For example, the 1929 market crash begot the Security and Exchange Commission.

Using the past as an indicator of the future, new regulations usually provide a blend of specific directives targeted at the known ways of failure, coupled with some vagueness or room for interpretation, as an attempt to predict what could happen next.

Although federal laws are enacted by legislative action of the U.S. Congress, the overall framework comprises federal, state, and local governments and the mandates that each of these levels of government enact. For example, Colorado has enacted cyber-security regulations.[3] In addition to regulatory mandates, very important industry-driven initiatives have the effect of regulations, such as the Payment Card Industry Data Security Standards[4] (PCI DSS). Each initiative carries enforcement mechanisms such as fines, citations, or, in the case of some industry initiatives (such as PCI DSS), restrictions on critical business operations (for example, processing credit card transactions).

Regulatory Approaches

When writing regulatory legislation, a governing body is faced with a significant challenge. If the regulation is too detailed and prescriptive, some organizations may be able to comply with the letter of the law while acting in a manner contrary to the spirit of that law. Conversely, the regulation may be too generic and vague, focusing on the legislation's intent or the end goal without being prescriptive about what a company must do to achieve compliance. In this case, interpretation of a regulation's requirements is difficult and subject to widely diverging opinions about what those requirements actually are. In general, the more detailed a regulation is, the easier it is to tell if an organization isn't in compliance.

---

[3] Colorado Office of Cyber Security, http://www.colorado.gov/cybersecurity (accessed 1 December 2009).

[4] PCI Security Standards Council, PCI DSS, https://www.pcisecuritystandards.org/security_standards/pci_dss.shtml (accessed 1 December 2009).

Vague regulations make it challenging to assess whether an organization is in compliance.

Regulators take two general approaches in drafting regulations. A *prescriptive approach* generally focuses on the letter of the law and contains reasonably specific requirements as to *how* you would go about complying with the regulation. This approach makes compliance more of a black-and-white issue, but it creates a risk that an organization could reasonably claim compliance with the letter of the law, while violating its spirit.

A *principle-based approach* generally relies on general principles and attempts to communicate what a reasonable person would do under similar circumstances. This approach is more likely to emphasize the end result that is desired (for example, an accurate financial statement) rather than the *means* required to achieve it. In some cases, a combination of these approaches may be used for a given regulation. For an example of how different regulations take different approaches, see "Example: SOX vs. HIPAA" in this chapter.

EXAMPLE: SOX VS. HIPAA

Let's look at two examples to see the difference in approach and results. One of the most important pieces of legislation of recent years has been the Sarbanes-Oxley Act of 2002. Despite good intentions, this law has created not only significant costs for many companies but also some uncertainty about what it requires for compliance. Section 404, in particular, has caused substantial process changes for public companies, which have been exacerbated by the law's lack of specificity.

Section 404 is only about 170 words long, but it has caused massive internal change for many large organizations. The point of this section is that it requires public companies to have *adequate internal controls to assure the correctness of corporate financial statements.* In order to resolve the ambiguity contained in that phrase, some companies adopt industry best practices, such as the Committee of Sponsoring Organizations of the Treadway Commission (COSO) framework or Control

Objectives for Information and related Technology (COBIT), to bring their processes into compliance with the law.

A different approach was adopted for HIPAA, which is much more prescriptive than SOX. As a result, HIPAA has generally caused less confusion, because its requirements are more specific than those in SOX.

The difference between a prescriptive and a principle-based approach to regulation can be illustrated in a hypothetical approach to compliance by a bank. Consider a financial regulation that states that if a loan is for a period greater than one year, a reserve fund must be established. Let's further assume that this bank routinely writes a loan with a term of 364 days and then rolls the loan over as another loan with a term for 364 days. A prescriptive approach might say that a reserve fund doesn't need to be established because the loan is for less than 365 days. A principle-based approach might say that this loan is effectively for more than 365 days and a reserve must be established.

A Regulatory Model

In Chapter 3, we explored the policy life cycle and showed how it can be used to create a continuous process of risk and compliance management across the organization. We discussed the fact that internal policy requirements are generally determined by a combination of corporate business objectives, regulatory requirements, and enterprise risks. Policies are then created to meet these requirements, and controls are implemented to ensure compliance with the policies. In general, as controls are tested, failure rates are measured; remediation may become necessary when these rates are outside the acceptable tolerance levels. As controls exhibit errors, the associated risks should be modified so that the current risk profile is current and accurate.

In theory, this is a simple model. In reality, it's very difficult to create a smoothly running continuous process such as this. A complete regulatory compliance program should include two other important areas: anomaly detection and training/awareness programs. Figure 9-1 depicts the expanded policy life cycle.

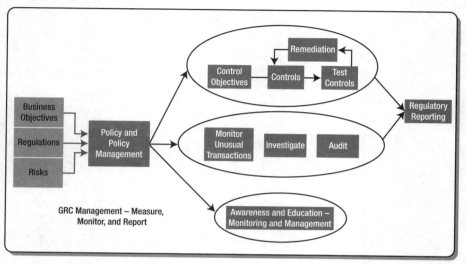

Figure 9-1. Regulatory compliance program components

When you deposit money into your bank account, the bank has a number of processes and internal controls to make sure the transaction is processed successfully. Generally, the signature is checked, the amount is checked against the available balance, and sometimes your identity is checked in person—all of these are basic controls in check validation and processing. But *anomaly detection* relates to finding transactions that don't fit normal patterns and may indicate a problem, such as fraud or money-laundering. For example, if you deposited $5,000 into your checking account, it's unlikely that any warning flags would be raised. However, if you did this every day for three months, it's possible that these cumulative transactions would be reported to some governmental authority. "Unusual transactions" or "transaction anomalies" are detected according to complex algorithms used by the banks or banking regulatory agencies. These events are also part of their compliance infrastructure because this information may need to be reported in a timely way to regulatory bodies.

Regulation Awareness

A comprehensive compliance infrastructure should include awareness, education, and processes. To prove compliance with a given regulation, you may need to show that your relevant employees have been trained in the regulation, that they understand and accept their obligations under it, and possibly that they have been tested and have sufficient knowledge of the regulation to comply with it.

Some regulations focus primarily on the need for awareness campaigns only, whereas others are much more demanding and require knowledge-testing and possibly periodic retraining.

For example, employees may be periodically notified via email and intranet announcements of their requirement to take part in computer-based compliance training. These training modules can be accompanied by short tests and deadlines. Participation in the training, as well as the cumulative scores of all employees may be recorded for compliance reporting purposes.

Key Strategies to Manage Regulatory Compliance

Regulatory compliance is a major challenge for most organizations and has also become a significant function within these organizations, requiring them to establish a centralized compliance effort, perhaps organized under a Chief Compliance Officer. Many companies have moved past the "check the box" approach to compliance and are moving toward building comprehensive compliance frameworks to simplify and streamline their compliance processes across the enterprise. They have realized that an effective and efficient compliance framework can be a competitive advantage, and they view it as a way to help improve the way their business operates as a whole. See the example in this chapter, "Case: The State of Colorado Department of Human Services."

CASE: THE STATE OF COLORADO DEPARTMENT OF HUMAN SERVICES

The State of Colorado Department of Human Services' (CDHS) compliance load is a heavy one. It must contend with the federal Health Insurance Portability and Accountability Act (HIPAA), various federal and state regulations, nearly 20 state cyber-security policies, and other IT mandates. As Colorado's second largest agency, CDHS has an annual operating budget of $1.8 billion, employs more than 5,000 employees, and works with thousands of community-based service providers. The department also oversees the state's 64 county departments of social and human services, including mental health and developmental disability services, the juvenile corrections system, and all state and veterans' nursing homes.

Within CDHS are numerous IT teams, each specializing in a unique technology management area, such as network security, engineering, messaging, and network and applications. Coordination among these teams can sometimes be less than optimal, according to Kelley Eich, chief technology officer for the CDHS: "At any given moment, if there's an incident or deviation from our policy, we could have four separate teams taking action, each without knowing what the others are doing," she explains. "When it comes to effectively and efficiently seeing and managing risks, this creates challenges."

That's no small management burden, considering that the agency must contend with 50 rules from HIPAA alone that govern the use of certain IT systems. To better manage these IT policies and their associated risks, CDHS last year licensed CA GRC Manager. "It comes with pre-populated choices," Eich says, "such as those that relate to our HIPAA mandates. Having those criteria already available helps us to better manage these efforts right out of the box." Over time, she adds, the CDHS will augment the solution with policies, procedures, and standards that are specific to its agency and business objectives.

The overall goal, Eich explains, is to streamline risk- and governance-related projects and teams, as well as to aggregate IT policies as they relate to various regulations and internal security and governance policies. "As the solution is deployed," she adds, "we will be able to make sure that our various departments are better focused on risk remediation, and we will have a more complete view of our risk posture at any given time."

Several factors about the regulatory environment and compliance are relevant to organizations looking to build effective compliance frameworks:

- Compliance with multiple regulations is complex for many reasons: lack of specificity, over-specificity, redundancy with other regulations, conflict with other regulations, and subjectivity of auditor/regulator, among others.

- Compliance with multiple regulations is expensive: demonstrating compliance is often, among other things, an exercise in evaluating and establishing controls, testing the controls on an appropriate basis, recording results and corresponding evidence, and potentially remediating failures. Add in audit preparation, audit participation, reporting compliance status, and compiling an overall perspective for executive management, and you have a time-intensive, costly proposition on your hands.

- Throwing people at the problem generally doesn't work in the long term and may foster and entrench the silos that contributed to the cost and redundancy in the first place. The PCI team cares about PCI, the SOX team cares about SOX, and so on. This approach satisfies the need for successful individual compliance initiatives, but does little to build a successful overall compliance program.

- Executive management may want a dashboard view of the organization's overall risk and compliance posture. Failure is not an option. This is clear to anyone who is responsible for compliance. The threat of fines, jail time, citations, bad publicity and resulting loss of reputation and business doesn't allow for half measures.

- The current regulatory climate will only increase pressure and complexity. It's often these very pressures that create and sustain a more ad hoc approach, creating silos of efforts and keeping even the most well-organized compliance initiatives and programs at a lesser level of maturity than could be achieved.

When you're attempting to address these issues and adopt a comprehensive approach to regulatory compliance, you should consider a number of guidelines or concepts. The following sections highlight some key strategies to facilitate an effective compliance regimen.

Get Involved Before Regulations Are Adopted

The entire regulatory process can be long and complex. Often, hearings are held to identify the regulation's key goals and requirements. A federal government agency may also meet with companies and stakeholders to craft the regulation's requirements. A draft regulation is submitted for public comment. The draft regulation and comments received during the review period are often published on the Internet. Based on the input, the regulation may be redrafted, and other documents may be produced that describe changes made (or not made) and the corresponding justifications.

This extended regulatory life cycle provides a good opportunity for companies to proactively attempt to either influence the content of these mandates or get a jump-start on compliance, so as to have a potential competitive advantage.

It's also helpful for companies to be proactive in their response to regulation by tracking areas where regulations may be emerging. Consider examining speeches given by regulators and politicians to get an idea of potential regulations, following industry periodicals that focus on impending legislation that may impact you, and tracking emerging regulations on the Internet, so that you can determine whether areas will be particularly problematic for your company or for other companies in your market. If so (and if you have the resources to devote to it), you may be able to influence the development of these regulations in an effort to head off these problems. Even if you cannot influence the regulation during the regulatory process, a proactive approach will often make you more prepared when you begin your compliance initiatives.

Transparency Is the Key to Success

The financial crisis that emerged in 2008 highlighted the key role of transparency in both compliance and risk management. Transparency doesn't guarantee that there will be no cases of corporate fraud or poor risk management. But the lack of adequate transparency does guarantee that if these situations occur, they're unlikely to be detected or corrected in a timely manner.

In layman's terms, *transparency* implies that the operation of your company is visible to the people who have a need and a right to have insight into it. Shareholders, corporate executives, regulatory agencies, and auditors are examples of groups that need certain levels of visibility into your operations. Some constituencies (shareholders) have limited visibility, and others (auditors) need substantially more detailed views into your internal processes and operations. Managing the tradeoff between corporate transparency and the appropriate management of information that could be a competitive advantage is always a difficult challenge.

As an example, consider a bank that has created a control framework that is used to manage enterprise risk. It needs to be set up in such a way that regulators can evaluate the effectiveness of these risk management processes. Auditors often compare your internal controls and processes to industry best practices. Without a level of transparency, they won't be able to fully understand your controls or compare them to other industry leaders. If they cannot fully analyze your controls, they may not be able to attest that you comply with regulations.

In the future, transparency-based compliance will probably continue to gain in importance. We have already seen evidence of this in the Standard & Poor's corporate evaluations, which now include evaluations of risk management approaches as part of their final ratings. It has become clear that in some cases, poor risk management practices can have a significant affect on a company's ability to repay its debt, which is precisely the focus of these corporate credit ratings. As a result, Standard & Poor's (as well as other rating agencies) has started to look at risk management practices in order to incorporate them into the final corporate ratings. In this case, poor transparency or poor risk management can have a decided financial impact on the corporation, because a lower S&P rating generally means higher borrowing costs.

Understand Your Transnational Regulation Issues

Compliance with U.S. laws and regulations is a major challenge. But take that challenge and expand it across many countries and regions of the world, some of which have overlapping or even conflicting regulations, and the challenge of global compliance becomes clear.

As an example, the European Union (EU) has laws that, in essence, create a single market through the union of its 27 member countries. Due to the concept of subsidiarity, the laws of the individual countries, unless found to be inadequate, prevail over EU law.[5] Therefore, a company doing business in an EU member country must conform to and be mindful of the laws of both the member country and the laws of the EU.

In some cases, the rules in one country may not legally apply to another country—but there is still great pressure to comply. For example, the Solvency II[6] directive, which is an updated set of regulatory requirements for insurance firms, applies to EU insurance companies but doesn't apply to the U.S. However, some U.S. insurance companies are being asked whether they comply with Solvency II; therefore, compliance with Solvency II has become a business imperative for some U.S.-based insurance companies.

To make this even more of a challenge, sometimes the laws and regulations of individual countries are inconsistent with those promulgated by the EU, making it very difficult for organizations acting across borders.

---

[5] Treaty on European Union, European Union, 29 July 1992, http://eur-lex.europa.eu/en/treaties/dat/11992M/htm/11992M.html (accessed 1 December 2009).

[6] Solvency II, European Commission, http://ec.europa.eu/internal_market/insurance/solvency/index_en.htm (accessed 1 December 2009).

There is no one best way for companies to organize their compliance efforts to minimize these challenges. Regulatory experts should be in place for any country in which an organization operates, and a central compliance group should be chartered with consolidating the requirements of these different countries and creating an enterprise-wide compliance strategy. Also, these regional compliance differences make it even more important that emerging regional regulatory requirements be closely monitored so that a company isn't surprised when a new regulation is enacted.

Automate Compliance Management

The previous strategies deal, for the most part, with advocacy and preparation. Investing in a management solution is a strategy unto itself, but is also an effective way to facilitate the strategies that follow and utilize the results gained from implementing those strategies.

Compliance, like any other discipline, needs to be managed. Spreadsheets, ad hoc databases and other disconnected tracking mechanisms are just that: *tracking mechanisms.* Home-grown solutions may become unwieldy and expensive to maintain and often lag behind regulatory changes.

The most effective management solution offers a balance of capabilities that delivers in three ways:

- *Satisfying the most pressing specific initiative:* Every organization has a *niche user*—the person with the most pressing and potentially painful compliance initiative on the horizon. You may lose credibility with them if your management solution cannot meet the most pressing and immediate need.

- *Flexibility*: With respect to capability number one, the solution cannot be so narrow as to work for only one regulation. A good architecture provides functionality for compliance that allows the user to define the type of compliance to be managed (PCI DSS, MAR, Gramm-Leach-Bliley Act [GLBA], SOX, J-SOX, and so on).

- *Satisfying the larger corporate programs that cover compliance, risk, policy management, and internal audit directives*: An excellent architecture provides a multipurpose solution that offers capabilities within each of the major categories of governance, risk, and compliance (GRC). Executive management and the Board want the overall GRC perspective—anything else is likely to spawn the need for a replacement solution down the road.

Centralize Compliance Information

Given these challenges of global compliance, it's important that information and processes related to the overall compliance program be centralized to avoid duplicated and often conflicting information, redundant effort, and high costs. Centralizing the most important compliance information, including cross-referencing that information to related risks and controls, helps bring order to compliance chaos and refocus on management strategies that help reduce or eliminate the redundant compliance silos across the organization. It also makes it much easier to get a clear picture of your total compliance posture at any point in time.

Centralized management of compliance also makes it much easier to accommodate the various needs of major regulations such as SOX, PCI DSS, HIPAA, and GLBA, which established new regulations for the financial services industry. Centralizing these requirements makes it easier to create a unified compliance platform, rather than create controls and activities highly specific for each regulation. You can often use the same controls for different regulations, saving time and money.

Figure 9-2 illustrates the use of the Unified Compliance Framework (UCF), a repository of controls for all major regulations, standards, and best practices across a range of industries. By using this repository, you can develop a rationalized set of controls to meet the requirements of a number of regulations, thereby eliminating duplication of highly overlapping controls. The columns represent specific regulatory or industry mandates, and the rows represent specific controls that are required by each one. As you can see, the ability to meet the needs of multiple regulations with a single control can be a significant benefit to your compliance program.

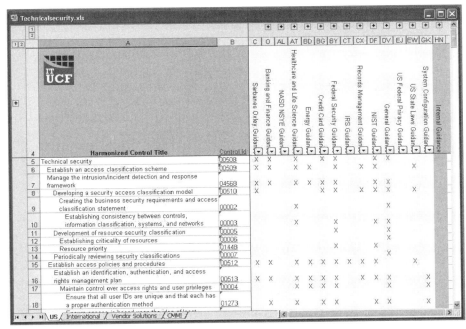

Figure 9-2. This UCF matrix maps controls to regulations[7]

Another driver to centralize compliance information relates to the challenge of project and program management across multiple compliance initiatives. Many activities are necessary to comply with regulations that are date driven. There are forms to fill out and checklists to be reviewed, all typically run by silos within the organization. It is often preferable for an organization to establish a common calendar and a common project management approach to regulations to understand what needs to be done for the next one to two years.

---

[7] Unified Compliance Framework, UCF Spreadsheets, http://www.unifiedcompliance.com/it_impact_zones/unified_compliance_framework_s.html (accessed 1 December 2009).

There will always be some cases where compliance information and activities are localized to a single, highly focused group. Examples are activities related to technical areas such as food and drugs or environmental regulations. You may find that centralizing this information completely isn't worth the added effort or cost; but most times, when significant potential for compliance information within silos exists, a centralized, unified approach to that compliance area is preferable.

Get the Right Information to the Right People

It's not enough to centralize compliance and/or risk information. Unless executives and managers can view this information in a way that is appropriate for their needs, its value will be diminished. Managers need *up-to-date, actionable information* that they can use to guide their decisions.

This creates a strong need for role-based dashboards and reports that provide at-a-glance, real-time information. These tools help managers determine their precise compliance posture, on both a regulation and organizational basis. They can also more quickly identify areas of emerging noncompliance. Managers can then drill down to the detail level, and assign other managers to initiate corrective action.

Customization is critical for the unique needs of each person. A plant manager can see the plant's compliance status, business managers can view it for their entire business, and the CEO can see the organization's overall compliance and risk posture.

Figure 9-3 is a simple example of a dashboard that executives can use to view the organization's current risk posture. It highlights the key emerging risks, so that corrective action can be taken quickly.

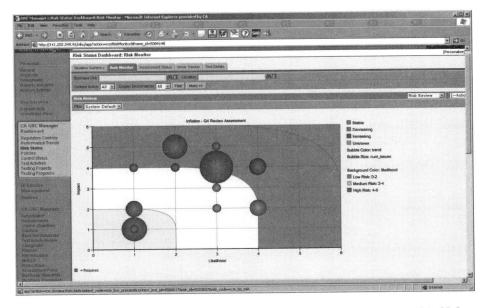

Figure 9-3. An executive dashboard of risk information, such as this example from CA GRC Manager, improves decision-making

The format of this dashboard display is less important than the fact that it provides the information that each individual needs, in a format that supports effective decision-making. It should provide not only current information but also historical trending information and analysis, so that it's easy for executives to see whether risks are increasing.

Secure Executive Support

As previously stated, you can build small wins and demonstrate success by providing comprehensive views of single initiatives at first, followed by additional initiatives and ultimately a comprehensive program. Providing visibility where none exists validates the investment in getting the management of compliance under control.

Conclusion

We have entered an environment where meeting the requirements of a range of regulations, as well as internal policies and industry mandates, is more important than ever. It's not enough to track each individual initiative and mitigate failures to a specific regulation. A strong management approach that leverages commonalities, depends on rationalized controls, creates efficiencies, and utilizes a centralized planning, tracking, and reporting mechanism, can improve your overall compliance posture.

Past and well-publicized infractions have resulted in increased regulations and greater scrutiny. Prepare to survive and thrive in this environment with a thorough understanding of what the regulations require and what controls are needed. Ensure consistent rationalized controls across regulations to not only manage costs but also enable you to react quickly to new regulations. Centralize and cross-reference your risk and compliance information so that it's always available and updated—this is the information on which executives may base their strategic business decisions. Pay particular attention to the challenge of global compliance, because conflicting or overlapping regulations can pose a major challenge. And finally, use your compliance initiatives to help establish a culture of ethical behavior and compliance to improve the overall effectiveness of the enteprise.

Governance and Finance

by Nancy E. Cooper and Alan Srulowitz

Governance and finance necessarily work hand in hand to help ensure that a company is sustainable during even the most challenging economic environments. This chapter looks at the important role governance plays in the arena of finance.

As we've discussed, governance establishes the culture, policies, procedures, and processes that form a structure within which companies are managed. In doing so, governance achieves at least two primary goals:

- To create value for the corporation

- To create transparency in the organization's operations

Executive management and the Board of Directors institute value and transparency by adopting proper company policies that clearly delineate a structure of authority, responsibility, and accountability for every process within the company—and by creating a system that helps ensure proper oversight.

The finance organization is a valued business partner for executive management and the Board of Directors, providing financial expertise, financial insight, and integrity, and thus the guidance needed to make decisions based on solid financial principles.

The Role of Finance

Finance has a role similar to, but different from, that of corporate governance. The similarities have to do with creating value and fostering transparency throughout the company. However, there are differences in the way the financial organization achieves value and transparency compared with corporate governance.

Value is added by developing and implementing effective enterprise planning that delivers data to stakeholders throughout the company. This is made possible by the finance organization's processes and systems. These processes and systems gather and assemble data into accurate and timely reports that are made available to internal and external stakeholders, enabling each to make decisions based on solid information.

Transparency is brought about by instituting systems and tools to deliver effective financial controls or governance for all company transactions. Financial controls enable stakeholders to review any aspect of a transaction with the least amount of effort and respond to potential deviation from policies and procedures in a timely manner. This enables management to monitor and measure the performance of aspects of the organization and to perform risk-based analytics to help managers make decisions.

Compliance tracking is a key element of systems designed by the company's financial organization. An ever-growing list of laws, regulations, and standards—in which violations may result in civil and, in some cases, criminal penalties—influence how a company operates. The financial organization provides expertise to help ensure that the company remains compliant by systematically monitoring the company's ongoing activities.

Traditional Finance

The financial organization is charged with many of the traditional functions you normally think of in association with finance. These include general accounting, revenue recognition, financial consolidation, and external reporting.

Other controls that fall under the finance umbrella include cash management and disbursements, including payroll and treasury management. Treasury management is critical to a solid foundation for company growth. Among the key treasury management responsibilities are designing the company's capital structure by balancing corporate debt with stock issuance and share repurchases. Treasury management also helps manage risk for the company in areas such as foreign currency risk management, and maintaining banking and rating agency relationships.

Tax management and analysis by the financial organization is another traditional responsibility and a critical element in returning value to the shareholder. In this role, the financial organization seeks to maintain a low effective tax rate through foreign and domestic tax planning. This helps ensure tax compliance at all levels while maximizing cash flow from taxes and from international subsidiaries.

The financial organization is also a steward of forecasting, budgeting, long-term planning, and performance analysis throughout the company. This provides accurate, consistent, and relevant information to management on a timely basis, forming the foundation for data-driven business decisions.

The Evolution of Finance

A new way of doing business has begun to take root in corporate finance organizations. We feel that modern finance organizations should establish rules for designing, managing, and monitoring financial processes that help ensure the value and transparency required by good corporate governance. A critical aspect of modern finance is to make sure the company's planning processes align with the organization's plans and with the company's strategic plan.

This alignment focuses stakeholders on the objective set by executive management and the Board of Directors, which decreases opportunities for segments of the organization to expend resources on activities that don't increase the bottom line.

Another activity of the modern finance organization is stewardship of acquisition of new entities by the company. Specifically, this amounts to effectively integrating the acquisition into the daily operations of the company and mitigating operational and financial risks related to the acquisition. This is particularly critical with multinational acquisitions that generate new regulations for the organization.

We believe a similar effort should be initiated whenever the company is exposed to new laws, regulations, and standards, regardless of national origin. A goal for the modern finance organization is to prepare the enterprise to revise existing policies and procedures to comply with new regulations.

As the role of Finance evolves, it has greater responsibilities for contingency planning for the company. *Contingency plans* are strategic and tactical roadmaps the company will follow in reaction to changes in business drivers, such as economic decline and system and control failures.

Managing Interdependencies

Growing interdependencies throughout the enterprise should include the finance organization. Governance also helps to manage interdependencies within finance functions to help ensure aggregate optimization of business decisions and organizational structure. This is a much different landscape than you find in many of today's companies, where decisions are made within silos throughout the company rather than being based on networking with other company entities.

For example, we've noticed that numerous forecasting processes occur within a finance organization. For example, the Financial Planning and Analysis group may forecast profit and losses. The Treasury group may forecast cash requirements for the organization. The Tax group may forecast expected tax rates and cash from taxes.

Good governance requires that all groups use common assumptions and source data. Where possible, the forecasting processes are based on each group's forecast or forecasting process. This mitigates the common risk of duplicating forecasting processes and basing multiple forecasts on different assumptions. It also leads to greater efficiencies by sharing resources and avoiding cost duplication.

Interdependencies should also be considered when the finance organization rolls out a new policy. The finance organization should consider the ramifications to all geographical locations, all functions within the company, and existing systems.

Let's consider a change in the travel and expense policy. Suppose the change delegates authority to managers to manage their employees' travel expenses and requires those managers to ensure that employees are compliant with the travel policy. Prior to this change, travel expenses and compliance were centrally managed by a group within the finance organization.

Governance needs to be in place to help ensure that the modified travel policy addresses local country requirements, meets legal requirements in all countries where the company operates, and provides managers with tools necessary to manage travel expenses for their employees.

Guiding Optimization of Decisions

The finance organization should assist all groups with making strategic and investment decisions. Each of these decisions should optimize the company's return on investment within the company's risk appetite. Furthermore, Finance should monitor the results of those decisions and recommend modifications to plans, should the results begin to fall from their forecasted mark. In addition, good governance requires that decisions follow a formal process based on predefined authority and responsibilities.

The role of governance within the finance organization is to provide assurance that every process has predefined rules specifying how the process is designed, managed, and monitored. These rules should specify the intersections with other processes throughout the company.

The goal is to have streamlined processes that are transparent throughout the company. When something happens in Tax, Treasury, or Mergers and Acquisitions, for example, its financial implications can be immediately understood by the finance organization. There are no surprises, such as cost overruns or control failures. No group within the company works in a vacuum.

Creating Intersections

All intersections of processes should be properly identified and reflected in the company's policies and procedures. This is a difficult task. The objective is to design processes to capture interdependencies and to have procedures in place that remediate gaps in interdependencies as soon as those gaps are identified.

Finance needs a central body within its organization that is responsible for managing, maintaining, and monitoring financial policies and procedures. Without a central body and repository for policies and procedures, there is a risk of duplicate efforts and having gaps in the inventory of policies and procedures.

The finance organization also needs to either manage or participate in the company's enterprise risk management program. This aligns decision-making criteria with the company's risk appetite and draws the focus of the finance organization to the analysis of higher risk areas of the company.

Internal controls over financial reporting for the Sarbanes-Oxley Act of 2002 (SOX) compliance should be managed, maintained, and/or monitored by the finance organization. This helps ensure that any remediation to procedures is effective and completed in a timely manner.

Unforeseen events may cause the company to shift strategies to avoid enterprise-wide business disruptions. Therefore, the finance organization should actively monitor the company's performance using robust analytics to help ensure that such events are managed based on accurate data and in a timely manner, so they don't disrupt the company's business model.

Goals of the Finance Organization

Key objectives of a finance organization can include the following:

- Effect enterprise planning

- Implement systems/tools to provide data accurately and transparently to internal stakeholders and enable efficient processing of transactions

- Deliver accurate and timely reports for internal and external stakeholders

- Effect financial controls and compliance

- Monitor and measure performance

- Provide value-added, risk-based analytics

To achieve these goals, the finance organization should have the right people, the right processes, and the right technologies in place. This is all brought about by governance. Good governance creates the environment and structure to manage the right people and processes. This can be achieved by doing the following:

- Ensuring that clear roles and responsibilities exist within the company so that employees know what they have to do and how to do it, and are aware that colleagues throughout the company are depending on their success.

- Holding everyone in the company accountable for the execution of procedures and controls. Results are graded as a team. The whole team fails if results aren't achieved.

- Setting the right tone throughout the company to help ensure that execution of processes is performed at optimal levels in a controlled environment.

Creating the Proper Environment

Corporate governance creates an environment and structure where processes are managed by ensuring that financial controls are built into applicable policies and procedures. The finance organization recommends financial controls to help ensure transparency of procedures that are associated with each policy and provide an objective mechanism for monitoring the execution of procedures.

This is made possible by producing standardized, accurate, and timely financial reports at all levels of management, enabling managers to know when to alter plans to accommodate failing processes before the failure can affect the bottom line.

The environment also requires an effective planning cycle. Every part of the company should use the same quality analytics to forecast business needs and develop a budget that allocates sufficient financial resources so those needs are met. This can help ensure that time-tested, risk-based decision making, guided by the financial organization, is effectively used by every manager in the company.

The proper governing environment requires that no policy or procedure be cast in stone. Good governance must foster the desire among managers to reduce inefficiencies and optimize standardization. Toward this end, company leaders should encourage everyone in the organization to assess current processes with best practices on an ongoing basis.

Managing Technologies

At the heart of every strong organization is a solid framework where technology is managed throughout. Technology is the company's nerve center, tying together all operations regardless of where they are in the world. Technology is also the tool that applies policies, procedures, and controls to all levels of the company. It's the glue of interdependency.

To create a healthy technology environment, you should implement systems that are designed to optimize automation in a cost-efficient manner. Based on our experience, we feel that as many processes should be automated as possible, with monitoring controls embedded within the process. A critical benefit of this is the assurance that the company remains compliant even given the expanding growth of laws, regulations, and standards that are imposed by governing bodies and industry groups throughout the world.

Properly implemented technology can provide global transparency when it comes to performance. Company leaders set global strategies within a risk appetite. Managers throughout the company implement business models that are designed to provide a desired return on investment to meet company objectives. Technology can then be utilized to monitor progress toward those goals by maintaining an electronic scorecard based on electronically captured data.

Systematizing Governance

Finance, as you've seen, plays a key role in the overall governance of the enterprise. As such, it follows and supports the governance approach adopted throughout the company. That is, Finance should set clear objectives and policies related to its charter and supported by its internal processes. Next, it should put in place controls that help ensure that these policies are followed as well as monitor them on an ongoing basis so that failures can be identified quickly. And, finally, it should define, measure, and monitor the risk associated with noncompliance with these policies.

The best way for Finance to do this is by embedding its governance principles within the organization's culture, processes, controls, and technologies. We call this *systematizing governance*. Whereas having separate governance rules can create an undesirable disconnect between governance goals and the actual functioning of the organization, the more that governance principles can be embedded within the organization's daily operation and processes—the more governance is systematized—the more likely it is that the governance goals of the enterprise will be met.

Transformation of the Finance Organization

In recent years, many finance organizations adopted an enterprise resource planning (ERP) system. This implementation required Finance to reengineer its processes by increasing standardization and, in many cases, centralizing activities. The ERP systems were designed to drive the retirement of multiple systems, spreadsheets, and databases. However, technology never stands still. New and improved technology is always over the horizon. To stay abreast with the marketplace, companies should continuously evaluate their ERP systems, pursue other technology solutions that complement ERP, and, in many instances, replace certain functionality within their system.

Technology can create a near-paperless environment, enabling greater workflow management and the building of efficient interdependencies among different departments, resulting in real-time processing that affects the entire company. Along with greater dependency on technology, companies are finding a greater need for good centralized governance to help ensure effective interdependency operations.

Technology also provides tools to non-financial managers so they can perform their own financial analysis. Decentralizing financial analysis has advantages, but it also increases the risk that the analysis is faulty. Good centralized governance is necessary to standardize roles and processes so that financial decisions are made consistently at all levels of the organization.

The matrix of multiple legal structures throughout the company's business units often leads to the formal or de facto formation of silos. Silos, as discussed earlier, have a tendency to inhibit communication and create inefficiencies through a complex organization. Technology, coupled with good centralized governance, tends to break down barriers between groups. This can be achieved by imposing and automatically enforcing standardization and transparency throughout the company.

Improved technology processing enables the finance organization's focus to transition from transaction processing to analytics. The finance organization helps to design and develop technology-based analytical tools that can be used by non-financial managers. They can then use the transparency provided by technology to closely monitor the performance of operating units throughout the globe. The finance organization role becomes more of an advisor and overseer than a group that processes transactions and aggregates budgets, all of which is now automated in the ERP system.

Keeping Pace in the Regulatory Race

Increased regulation from the Security and Exchange Commission (SEC) and newly introduced accounting pronouncements for generally accepted accounting principles (GAAP) are telltale signs of the regulatory changes expected as a result of the economic environment that emerged in 2008. Leading this charge is the new accounting mandate called International Financial Reporting Standards (IFRS).

A company's financial organization must map current accounting processes to IFRS to identify where they intersect and locate gaps. Gaps require that changes be made to the current accounting process in order to bring them in compliance with IFRS.

Mapping to IFRS is an opportunity for the finance organization to develop a proactive process that moves the organization to a more principle-based accounting model. Such an accounting model standardizes accounting processes throughout business units. This will make it easier in the future to map new regulations to current accounting processes and to modify the accounting process accordingly. At CA, we feel the best approach is to compare IFRS to current operations and current compliance efforts and determine where they overlap and what is new. Next, revise your policies and procedures to reduce redundancies in order to comply with new and existing regulations.

Under *rule-based* regulations, the regulations tell you (and the auditors confirm) the way the firm must recognize revenue based on standard accounting rules. In contrast, a *principle-based* regulation defines a goal and not specifically how that goal is reached. Adopting a more principled approached to accounting is critical to making changes to your current accounting and compliance processes as painless as possible.

IFRS is a principle-based regulation. Most companies, however, are currently following a rule-based accounting process. It's a major challenge for companies to map principle-based regulations to their rule-based accounting processes. Adding further complications is the very rules-based SEC. No one knows for sure how smoothly this transition will occur.

The principles didn't matter in the U.S. as long as rules were followed. Now, with IFRS, this is changing. The finance organization should now design an accounting process structure that can adhere to both principle-based regulation and rule-based regulation.

A Streamlined Approach Is Mandated

The current economic climate that surfaced in 2008 creates additional pressure to reevaluate cost structure and look for ways to streamline processes and costs. Governance plays a key role in this streamlining by providing mechanisms to anticipate changes to business drivers and give management the tools to develop contingency plans as market pressure intensifies.

We can only expect the rate and pace of change to increase in complexity. Therefore, it's imperative that governance within the organization as a whole, and especially within the finance organization, be structured so that management can detect and analyze these changes and efficiently develop a response that minimizes the impact to the business.

The finance organization governs itself the same way it contributes to corporate governance: by establishing a culture of transparency, accountability, and discipline through continuously improving the design, management, and monitoring of its policies and procedures.

To reach this goal, the finance organization embeds governance within all key processes of its business. Each process owner is responsible for the design, management, and monitoring of policies and procedures associated with the process. The process owner designs, manages, and monitors the financial controls that are integrated into the policies and procedures owned by the process owner.

However, you can't rely on the process owners to identify and manage interdependencies that exist across process owners. To address this issue, you should embed global processes in governance to help ensure that interdependent processes achieve the company's objectives.

Global processes can include at least the following:

- Budgeting and forecast monitoring

- A monthly close process to help ensure the accuracy of internal reporting

- Assessment of internal control over the financial reporting process

- A disclosure process that identifies and remediates potential subprocesses that must be compliance-certified

- Strategic decision processes

- Data processes to help ensure accurate data

- Business intelligence processes to help ensure that all managers are working with the same data and the same assumptions

Challenges and Opportunities

In today's world, finance organizations face many challenges. But these challenges are often opportunities to strengthen the company's sustainability even while facing a constant barrage of new laws and regulations.

If you apply the concepts in this chapter, your organization should employ a holistic approach to governance by breaking down silos that typically impede communication and lessen transparency. The key to implementing a holistic approach to governance is the development of an effective partnership between the finance organization and the IT organization, including the IT compliance group described in Chapter 7.

The IT organization consists of content experts who know the systems and data that run the company. They also have the skill set to design and build controls into existing and new systems that automatically impose and monitor compliance with policies and procedures throughout the company.

Through this partnership, the finance organization can shift its focus from transaction processing to transaction and data analysis, enabling employees to raise the level of their strategic thinking and providing managers with valuable insight into decision making. Automation standardizes reporting by making reporting a superset of operational reporting requirements. All reports used to monitor and manage business operations are standardized, enabling auditors and managers with oversight responsibilities to view the same reports used by management to make business decisions.

Conclusion

Governance must be embedded within financial processes. In this way, Finance can deliver on its mission to be recognized as a valued business partner through leadership in financial expertise, insight, and integrity, thus helping to enable a company to deliver superior results. Strong governance is also critical to help ensure the scalability of financial processes in an ever-changing environment.

Information Governance

by Galina Datskovsky, Ph.D., CRM

According to the Aesop's fable "The Ant and the Grasshopper," a grasshopper chirped and hopped the summer away as a neighboring ant toiled in the field, carrying kernel after heavy corn kernel to its nest. When the grasshopper asked the ant to stop and play, the ant replied, "Winter is coming, and I'm getting ready. I recommend you do the same." The grasshopper just laughed and said, "Why bother about winter? We have plenty of food today." When winter finally came, the grasshopper lay weak with hunger while the ant fed on the corn it had worked so hard to gather. The grasshopper realized too late that he should have prepared for a known risk.

Like the grasshopper, many organizations fail to anticipate and plan for the inevitable. They don't proactively address risks, and then they hope for the best. They're almost completely reactive in how they run their business. They fail to control and manage information as a valuable asset. They hope that discovery (the phase of a lawsuit in which parties can compel the production of documents and other evidence to "discover" pertinent facts) and external audits don't happen to them and that they don't accidentally lose or disclose information that is vital to the operation of the company. These companies have failed to embrace Information Governance (IG).

What they don't know about their information, and what they don't do to control and manage their information, can come back and bite them.

Information Governance Basics

Every day, companies must safeguard and precisely catalog millions of bits of data that encompass their corporate memory, their intellectual property, their corporate records, and the flow of information that is crucial for business operations—and is the organization's life blood. They must not only keep such data safe from hackers and crooks, but also enable executives to quickly find critical information within that data when a regulatory agency, accountant, lawyer, or business need demands it.

Information can include anything that an organization has compiled or its employees know. It can be stored and communicated. It covers a wide variety of data including customer information, proprietary information, and/or protected (for example, by copyright, trademark, or patent) and unprotected (such as business intelligence) information. Information also covers an ever-widening variety of formats including printed copies, computer files, and databases.

Information should be managed with the same level of attention given to managing other valuable corporate assets. Many organizations focus their management efforts too narrowly on tangible *information assets*, which include the words and numbers that describe business entities such as inventory, customers, and finances. Just as important, but often overlooked, is the management of intangible information assets, such as those that describe company goals, processes, and relationships.

Information security generally refers to the confidentiality, integrity, and availability of information assets.

Corporate governance is the set of processes, customs, policies, controls, regulations, and institutions that affect the way a corporation is directed, administered, or controlled. Effective governance helps ensure that executives know what information resources are out there, what condition they're in, and what role they play in the success of the business. Executives also need to know what information or lack of information places the company at risk.

Therefore, IG is essentially the policies and procedures that a company uses to govern and control the use, access, analysis, retention, and protection of its information. Organization-wide IG policies define how information is controlled, accessed, and used. IG touches on everything from retention to deletion and from compliance and eDiscovery to integrity, reliability, and availability for business purposes.

The essence of IG is implementing and managing common policies and controls regarding the organization's information assets across the enterprise.

IG has three core objectives:

- Provide more transparency and better information management visibility, thereby achieving higher operational performance and better overall governance.

- Achieve consistency in information compliance across today's large, complex enterprises, which span many regulatory environments and geographies.

- Produce an ongoing record of the organization's information-management processes. This provides documentary evidence of how information is managed over time.

Effective IG integrates an organization's information processes and life cycles with its overall governance policies and controls.

The Components of Information Governance

IG is made up of the following interrelated concepts:

- Email archiving

- eDiscovery

- Compliance

- Federated Records Management (FRM)

Email archiving generally refers to applications that copy or remove email from the mail server and manage it in a central location known as an *archive*.[1] Information technology professionals use the term *archiving* to mean the copying or transfer of files for storage. In general, these applications collect email from all designated users (aka custodians) in a central repository (which may include attachments, calendars, task lists, and so on). Email-archiving applications typically require little or no action on the part of the user to store or manage the email records. After messages are stored, authorized users are able to search the repository.

Depending on the company and its business purposes, email-archiving applications may provide the following benefits. Each application has different features and different strengths, so this list is not exhaustive:

- More efficient storage of email, because the email is moved from a distributed network of servers, desktop applications, and other locations to be centrally managed

---

[1] National Archives and Records Administration, NARA Bulletin 2008-05, 31 July 2008, http://www.archives.gov/records-mgmt/bulletins/2008/2008-05.html (accessed 1 December 2009).

- Enhanced electronic search capability for content that may be germane to a subpoena, Freedom of Information Act request, eDiscovery request, or similar request

- Assistance with back-up and disaster recovery

eDiscovery refers to any process in which electronic data is sought, located, secured, and searched with the intent of using it as evidence in a legal case. It can be carried out offline on a particular computer, or it can be done in a network. Court-ordered or government-sanctioned investigation for the purpose of obtaining critical evidence is also a type of eDiscovery.

The nature of digital data makes it extremely well suited to such investigations. For one thing, digital data can be electronically searched with relative ease, whereas paper documents must be scrutinized manually. Furthermore, digital data is difficult or impossible to completely destroy, particularly if it gets into a network. This is because the data can appear on multiple hard drives and because digital files, even if deleted, may be able to be undeleted. In fact, the only reliable way to destroy a computer file is to physically destroy every hard drive where the file has been stored. In the process of electronic discovery, data of all types can serve as evidence. This can include text, images, calendar files, databases, spreadsheets, audio files, animation, websites, and computer programs.

The key to addressing eDiscovery is to be proactive in the management of information and records, with suitable control over the handling of potential eDiscovery requests.[2] Records management professionals must work with the legal staff and IT to develop a records and information management program that supports eDiscovery efforts. Records management policies and procedures must be developed, establishing strong records management discipline among employees in managing the business information and records they deal with. This policy should stress the following:

---

[2] Association for Information and Image Management, "What is e-Discovery?" http://www.aiim.org/What-is-eDiscovery.aspx, (accessed 1 December 2009).

- Information without business value should be disposed of according to policy and in the normal course of business.

- Records that have value to the organization must be stored and managed properly, under the control of the organization.

- A classification scheme providing an information and records management structure should be implemented for consistency and control.

- Records that are no longer needed should be destroyed in a systematic and documented way.

- Upon determination that litigation is reasonably likely to occur, the business must be able to effectively and efficiently suspend all record disposition procedures.

Compliance, in the corporate sense, is the obligation to meet defined requirements (internal and external rules) at specific times and maintain the records required to provide evidence of a company's conduct. Compliance aligns information management with corporate governance. This is accomplished by placing and managing controls on content, thus enabling a company to manage and mitigate potential risk of noncompliance. Compliance provides organizations with an improved ability to abide by and continuously monitor their adherence to ever-changing regulations, laws, court opinions, administrative rules, and interpretive guidance—including, for example, Sarbanes-Oxley (SOX), the Financial Industry Regulatory Authority (FINRA), the Health Insurance Portability and Accountability Act (HIPAA), the Data Protection Directive, and privacy mandates. Compliance also includes adherence to internal standards and policies as well as an alignment with both corporate best practices and recommended best practices from respected external standards bodies.

Federated Records Management (FRM) is an approach that essentially manages the processing of information across an organization through a determined life cycle based on business processes and controls, including established retention schedules. The information life cycle is governed by policies for content retention and IG. The purpose of FRM is threefold:

- To maintain consistency, efficiency, and transparency across all disparate information systems throughout the organization.

- To provide appropriate access to the information.

- To enforce the designated information life cycle.

With these three component elements, IG provides organizations with the ability to set proactive controls based on policies that can be both integrated into information systems and monitored on a continuous basis, thereby providing the requisite stable, repeatable infrastructure to assist in achieving successful governance of information throughout its life cycle. This approach assures that IG's activities are in accordance with relevant legal rules and regulations while conforming to prevailing best practices and ethical standards that frequently can go beyond legal compliance. IG therefore defines and controls the way organizations manage information.

Goals of Information Governance

Information is the life blood of any modern day business. Companies succeed or falter based on the reliability, availability, and security of their information. A great deal of organizational intellectual capital exists in the form of information assets. An organization's knowledge is stored in many different systems, such as email, document management applications, SharePoint portals, FTP sites, shared and personal drives, various databases, corporate intranets, and many more. According to the Enterprise Strategy Group (ESG),[3] as much as 70% of corporate intellectual property is stored within or is accessible via email.[4] Primary research from WinterCorp's "Winter TopTen Program" shows a consistent trend since 1998; the size of

---

[3] ESG Market Review, "Unlocking the True Power of Enterprise Message Management", September 2005.

[4] ESG Market Review, "Unlocking the True Power of Enterprise Message Management", September 2005.

the largest data warehouse they validate triples approximately every two years.[5]

These realities present an interesting set of problems to an organization. In order to conduct business effectively and in a manner compliant with regulatory and ethical policies, this information must be effectively governed. As you'll see in the pages that follow, there are many drivers for efficient IG. Let's list the goals of IG:

- Risk mitigation, defensible programs, and cost containment.

- Content protection, privacy and security enforcement, and the prevention of information leaks.

- Content control through consistent management across content silos via a policy authority, which is a directive issued by an organization in the form of a policy.

- Proactive evaluation of content to determine whether risk, cost, or inefficiency outweighs its value.

- Elimination of content based on approved retention schedules to improve efficiencies and reduce risk.

- Retention rules that specify the point in time at which content should be reevaluated or destroyed.

- Ensuring ready access to content independent of location, format, source, or status.

---

[5] *Why Are Data Warehouses Growing So Fast*, Richard Winter, 10 April 2008, http://www.b-eye-network.com/view/7188 (accessed 1 December 2009).

We'll next examine the drivers, cite some compelling reasons for embarking on the road to a better governance strategy, and provide a practical guide to getting started.

Driving Forces for Information Governance

Many forces drive the need for IG. Let's examine some of the major drivers.

Heavy regulatory and legislative pressures. Many industries have become accustomed to heavy regulations. For example, in the U.S., the financial industry has long been governed by Securities and Exchange Commission (SEC) regulations. Similarly, the pharmaceutical industry has long been subject to FDA regulations in the U.S. and to EudraLex (the rules governing medicinal products in the European Union) in Europe. In light of the economic crisis that emerged in 2008, many other industries may be subjected to heavier regulations as well as greater oversight. To comply with such regulatory requirements in a cost-effective and proactive manner, IG becomes essential.

Increased focus on transparency. Although transparency in corporate behavior and government has been important in the past decade, it became increasingly more so during the financial crisis which began in 2008. The Obama administration in the U.S. has been heavily emphasizing the need for transparency in government agencies. Why is transparency necessary? Together with authenticity of information, it helps promote trust in government agencies and corporate citizens. Take the case of Bernard Madoff,[6] the disgraced Ponzi schemer. He certainly had records that documented his business; however, his firm clearly lacked transparency (they wouldn't disclose how they arrived at their results) and authenticity of their results (no audit trail or metadata was available to prove the origin of the records). Think how much easier it would be for organizations to do business together if they agreed on what transparency and authenticity in

---

[6] U.S. Department of Justice, Southern District of New York, United States v. Bernard L. Madoff, http://www.justice.gov/usao/nys/madoff.html (accessed 1 December 2009).

business meant and if citizens and stakeholders could have a degree of trust in the organizations that subscribed to these policies. The only way to ensure such behavior is through a strategy that incorporates IG.

Corporate and individual accountability. Along with transparency and authenticity come corporate and individual responsibility and accountability. Many cases show that corporations as well as their senior management are held accountable for various actions, including the improper handling of information. We'll discuss this later in the chapter.

Security of information. If your company or agency has confidential or secure records, safeguarding the assets and potentially declassifying them on a set schedule becomes an imperative of a good governance initiative.

Defensible policies and procedures for all information. Because of the nature of audit and litigation readiness today, policies for IG must be clear and defensible either to an auditor or in a litigation or dispute.

Innovation-driven projects with fast results. Companies and government agencies want to deliver IG while capitalizing on their existing investments in technology. They want innovation, lower costs, and increased ROI. For example, if a corporation had a "keep all information forever" policy and can now start to dispose of information based on IG policies and procedures, increased efficiency and costs savings in terms of storage, servers, and staff—as well as cost savings during an audit or a litigation—can be realized.

Social Implications of Information Governance

After the housing/mortgage bubble burst in 2008, there is a greater drive to change the way businesses and governments operate. The drive is toward greater transparency, accountability, authenticity, and reliability. In fact, ARMA International, a not-for-profit, professional association and an authority on managing records and information, has developed a set of

Generally Accepted Recordkeeping Principles^{sm} (GARP ^{sm})[7] as a reflection of today's needs.

One natural consequence of any crisis is an increase in oversight and likely the enactment of more regulations. This likely translates to more complex records management requirements and retention policies, and tighter governance. You can also expect more litigation and therefore more discovery requests, making a consistent methodology for eDiscovery ever more essential. More rules and regulations are inevitable. More government transparency and accountability are also likely.

It has become increasingly apparent that in order to effectively conduct business, and in order to instill public and regulatory confidence, enterprises have to demonstrate that they operate in a transparent and auditable manner. Again, Bernie Madoff had records; but unfortunately, his business practices and his company's records lacked transparency and authenticity.

Any business or government agency that exercises control over its information assets can work in a more efficient and socially responsible manner. We predict that organizations that embrace good governance will win more business, retain their top talent, and have better social standing and a more positive public image. Good corporate governance involves six key social requirements:

- Transparency

- Accountability

- Due process

- Compliance

- Meeting statutory and common law requirements

---

[7] ARMA International, "ARMA International Challenges Organizations to Implement Better Recordkeeping: Announcing the Generally Accepted Recordkeeping Principles", http://www.arma.org/press/Pdf/GARP_Media_Release.pdf (accessed 1 December 2009).

- Security of personal information

Today's increasingly complex information and communication technology environments necessitate managing information within organizations and processes that span multiple administrative, legislative, political, organization, jurisdictional, conceptual, and social boundaries.

The Benefits of Good Information Governance

The goal of IG is to build a compliance and governance framework that provides proactive controls for the information and records that document an organization's business actions and decisions. Implementing IG provides an integrated approach to the processing of information. By centralizing policy enforcement for information-based applications, IG streamlines the ability of organizations to proactively stay in compliance with their operating policies—and thereby better achieve their legal and regulatory obligations. Further, by integrating policy enforcement into FRM, an organization's IG policies can provide global, corporate-wide consistency that simplifies FRM deployment.

The value, as well as the need, for IG is clearly identified in the findings of the 2007 Cohasset/ARMA/AIIM survey on electronic records management.[8] This is the fifth time Cohasset Associates conducted this research. The findings of this survey have come to be recognized as the definitive biannual statement of how well organizations are addressing the key issues associated with the management of electronic records. The conclusions of the latest survey are as follows:

> *"The majority of organizations are not prepared to meet many of their current or future compliance, legal, and governance responsibilities because of the deficiencies in the way they currently manage their electronic records."*

---

[8] Cohasset Associates, "Information Governance—A Core Requirement for the Global Enterprise," White Paper, October 2007.

*"The integration of electronic records into the organization's
records management program should be a priority, and
electronic records control gaps should be the focus of
immediate corrective action."*

*"A majority of organizations still are not doing what they
need to do regarding digital preservation - to ensure integrity
and future accessibility to their electronic records."*

*"Traditional communications barriers must be broken down
between stakeholders, and a new commitment to
collaboration concerning recordkeeping requirements and
retention management must take place."*

*"The outstanding challenges associated with the
management of electronic information assets have the
potential to be devastating in terms of costs, professional
careers, and even corporate reputations."* [9]

Probably the greatest reason to deploy IG is that it improves the
functionality and performance of existing records management systems and
more tightly ties their relationship to corporate governance and compliance.
With its innate capability to improve compliance and governance, IG
mitigates major information risks.

IG can also provide three significant cost-avoidance benefits:

*"Lower eDiscovery costs: Cohasset's research shows that
American businesses spend at least $2.5 to $4.0 million per
year for eDiscovery per billion dollars in sales. A company
with $20 billion in sales therefore spends between $25 and
$40 million annually on eDiscovery. For most organizations,
annual eDiscovery costs are now their second largest
uncontrolled expense, exceeded only by healthcare.*

---

[9] Cohasset Associates, "Information Governance—A Core Requirement for the Global
Enterprise," White Paper, October 2007, pages 2-3.

Accordingly, lower eDiscovery costs are a compelling basis for implementing IG. For many, this is a low-hanging fruit—an easy-to-achieve value." [10]

"Proactive preparation for litigation and audit: The Federal Rules of Civil Procedure (FRCP) are court procedures for civil suits in United States federal courts. The revised (2006) FRCP, as well as similar subsequent revisions of various state rules of civil procedure, with their focus on eDiscovery issues, provide a new rationale for implementing IG with its core commitment to enforcing information and records management policies—particularly for any company doing business in the U.S." [11]

"Higher standard of performance and greater consistency: The common call of lawmakers, regulators, and courts is for higher performance and greater consistency in the way information is managed and controlled. This makes IG the right solution at the right time. IG provides a needed solution to address one of the most challenging and significant information management problems of our time: mitigating two ever-present and very consequential risks: non-compliance and governance failures." [12]

Information Governance and Discovery

Another major driver for IG is preparedness for litigation and audit. In U.S. government agencies, discovery is also driven by the Freedom of

---

[10] Cohasset Associates, "Information Governance—A Core Requirement for the Global Enterprise," White Paper, October 2007, page 4.

[11] Cohasset Associates, "Information Governance—A Core Requirement for the Global Enterprise," White Paper, October 2007, page 4.

[12] Cohasset Associates, "Information Governance—A Core Requirement for the Global Enterprise," White Paper, October 2007, page 5.

Information Act (FOIA) and in Europe by Directive 2003/98/EC[13] and EC Regulation 1049/2001.[14] ARMA International has conducted surveys about the state of records management in various industries.[15] The surveys reveal that few organizations have appropriate "hold" mechanisms to ensure preservation of Electronically Stored Information (ESI). However, all relevant and reasonably accessible information must be produced in a timely manner, regardless of its potential to embarrass or damage.

Unfortunately, to date, few organizations have found a way to repeat the procedures required to reduce the costs and overall impact of discovery to the business. Large enterprises spend an average of $20 million per litigation for eDiscovery. Adding to this complexity, ESG estimates that as much as 70% of corporate intellectual property is stored in or accessible via email.[16] Quotas on email servers are resulting in end users moving more messages to local stores (such as PST files), which generally makes discovery and disclosure more difficult.

As you've seen in some of the previously mentioned cases, knowing the answers to the "what" and "where" questions are extremely important.

When focusing on litigation and response readiness, or during information disclosure exercises, a corporation should focus on ensuring defensibility and compliance and on lowering costs. Compliance can't start after a litigation strikes or a disclosure request is initiated. After such an event

---

[13] The Council and the European Parliament, Directive 2003/98/EC - Directive on the re-use of public sector information, http://ec.europa.eu/information_society/policy/psi/docs/pdfs/directive/psi_directive_en.pdf (accessed 1 December 2009).

[14] Regulation (EC) No 1049/2001 of the European Parliament and of the Council of 30 May 2001 regarding public access to European Parliament, Council and Commission documents, http://www.legaltext.ee/text/en/T50986.htm (accessed 1 December 2009).

[15] "Records Management Professionals Report their Email Management and eDiscovery are Not Under Control," Press Release, 20 October 2008, http://www.ca.com/us/press/release.aspx?cid=189590 (accessed 1 December 2009).

[16] ESG Market Review, "Unlocking the True Power of Enterprise Message Management", September 2005.

occurs, disposition must be suspended for all potentially relevant or responsive information. Therefore, organizations that engage in proactive management of information prior to any event occurrence can present a more defensible strategy around their information disclosure policies and practices.

Proactive management also leads to lowered costs. In the past, we've seen a trend toward outsourcing many of the response processes; but bringing many of these processes in-house may reduce costs and minimize the amount of content that needs to go through a review process. Based on better business practices, by eliminating duplicates and irrelevant information and disposing of information at appropriate times as permissible by law (absent a duty to preserve), discovery can be a more streamlined, repeatable, and simplified process.

Further, having a proactive IG strategy allows these special tasks to occur with minimal disruption to the business, IT, and end users. Imagine for a moment a discovery request where all users have arbitrary information on their laptops and most of the workforce is mobile. Now, imagine the difficulty you'd have collecting all information relating to a specific situation from all of those users. The costs and disruption associated with this process, if you had to do it once, would be large. Think of the cost if you had to repeat the process, as often happens, multiple times for various inquiries. Imagine all the resources that would be impacted and the time lost. Imagine the dollars spent. And imagine your confidence level in your current processes.

Now, imagine the same situation but with a clear policy; a map of what is kept and where it resides; appropriate controls in place that streamline information retention, disposition, and proper preservation; and clear governance definitions. A repeatable process allows for increased predictability and ease of response in terms of both efficiency and effectiveness.

Information Governance and Information Technology

One of the key themes of President Obama's election and presidential platform was transparency and accountability. What does that mean to the enterprise, and why does it make the need for cooperation between IT, legal, and records management so essential?

In today's world, with its demands for transparency, integrity, and auditability, it's increasingly important for organizations to ensure cooperation between their records/information management and IT practices. With greater government oversight, expected regulations, and Boards and shareholders that demand authenticity, an organization should ask itself how to make sure its information assets comply with the requirements of this new climate.

The natural place to turn is to the experts in records and information management for their know-how in structuring and appropriately protecting the information generated in their organizations. However, because most of an organization's transactions take place in electronic format, it's also essential to turn to the custodians of the information—the IT organization—to implement and audit business policies. These two organizations can't be successful today without a strong degree of cooperation or partnership. Legal must also be consulted and included as strategies evolve, to help ensure that the appropriate steps are taken in accordance with legal, compliance, and ethical requirements for any organization.

Although the IT organization is the custodian of information, transparency, auditability, and other business policies need to be set by the information owners. Defensible policy also results in consistent policy across all repositories and silos of information. Determining the implication of introducing new content silos and systems, and knowing legal and regulatory requirements, become essential parts of the duty of the custodian—the IT organization. Hence, the importance of teaming with the legal department. Similarly, information owners, in cooperation with the IT department, need to be concerned with data protection, a critical element of IG policies. In the world of regulation, privacy protection and information security play essential roles. Again, the IT organization needs to rely on business managers to understand the need for data protection in the various silos. For example, employee data requires a greater degree of protection and nonproliferation than certain marketing materials. This is where it's critical for the records management staff to step in with policy knowledge so that IT deploys and stores information in accordance with best practice principles.

Consider the many pressures facing the IT organization today. The business is constantly placing new demands for technology on the IT organization in order to work better, faster, and cheaper. Examples of such technologies can include social networking sites, blogs, and wikis. These technologies, if rolled out without consideration for governance, accountability, and transparency, can pose great dangers to the organization. Here is where IG can play a major role in advising IT on how to roll out the systems in the safest way for the organization.

IT is also under pressure to reduce costs. Appropriate recordkeeping practices allow organizations to safely dispose of information and, therefore, reduce storage and backup costs. Such practices also reduce the cost of eDiscovery, because the relevant information is easier to find and less information has to be examined by legal teams for relevance and review.

In short, the partnership between IT and records and information management (RIM) has never been more important than in today's business climate. An open dialogue and understanding between the two organizations, as well as other business owners and constituencies (such as legal), will produce better governance for the enterprise.

But how do you get these groups to talk to each other? Common vocabulary and understanding of each other's perspectives are key, but a formal process is also important.

Information Governance and Cloud Computing

IG is applicable to the use of cloud computing because we're basically defining the IT architecture as a set of services that are re-locatable between on-premises and cloud computing–based systems. The same principles, policies, and procedures that apply to these services are provided within the enterprise or on a cloud.

Your organization's policies in the context of cloud computing should be declarative electronic rules about what can be done with a service, to a service, and by whom. These include the following:

- Who can access the service

- Who can access the data in the service

- What they can do to the service

- What can they do with the data in the service

- How changes to the service and data affect other services and other data

- How changes to the service affect applications

- Basic security and data-access controls

- Links with services testing

- Service and data discovery

- Service and data delivery

- Service and disposition policies

- Policies on setting and maintaining appropriate service levels

- How to manage errors and exceptions

- Policies on enabling online upgrades and versioning

- Service and data validation

- Auditing and logging

An Information Government Framework

As IT organizations introduce new technologies, it's essential that they do so within the framework of IG. Consider, for example, the introduction of social media to engage in social networking discussions and information sharing through blogs, podcasts, videos, wikis, message boards, and online forums. What are the implications of employees engaging in social networking during business hours, using company equipment, and saving those communications on the organization's storage devices and backup media? What are the discovery obligations? How do you plan to capture the associated files and make them full-text searchable in the event of discovery? These questions should be answered before a technology is introduced into an environment.

To facilitate this practice, you should develop an IT questionnaire and go through it routinely with every new technology rollout or whenever you plan any strategic information decisions for the organization.

The ISO/IEC 38500:2008 standard[17] provides a framework for effective governance of IT to help those at the highest level of organizations to understand and fulfill their legal, regulatory, and ethical obligations with respect to their organization's use of IT. ISO/IEC 38500 is applicable to organizations of all sizes, including public and private companies, government entities, and not-for-profit organizations. This standard provides guiding principles for organizations on the effective, efficient, and acceptable use of IT within their organizations.

---

[17] International Organization for Standardization, "Corporate Governance of Information Technology," http://www.iso.org/iso/catalogue_detail.htm?csnumber=51639, (accessed 1 December 2009).

Seven Steps to Achieving Good Information Governance

What can you do to initiate an IG program in your organization? You need to make sure your business has a solid information strategy and commit to take steps to properly govern how your information is used, shared, and analyzed. Here are seven ways you can get started:

STEP 1 It's critical to understand the compliance regulations that govern your business. These may include, but aren't limited to, regulations; laws; industry standards, such as Department of Defense (DoD) 5015.2, International Organization of Standards (ISO) 15489, PRO (Public Records Office [UK]), and VERS (Victorian Electronic Records Strategy); and organizational best practices, such as the Quality Electronic Records Practices Specifications (QERPS) and Good Electronic Records Management (GERM) Parts 1 and 2 ("Complying with 21 CFR Part 11—Electronic Records and Electronic Signatures").

STEP 2 Build a team or task force to work on your policies and procedures. It should include not only your compliance officer and records manager but also IT and corporate counsel. Build and review records policies for retention and disposition, as well as discovery procedures for all corporate knowledge (records and non-records). Understand privacy, need-to-know limits, and FOIA impacts. Review your security infrastructure to secure information accordingly. For example, if you have sensitive documents such as HR information in email, and an HR professional moves to another department, do you have a way to secure the sensitive information that may be in his or her mailbox?

STEP 3 Identify IT challenges such as email disruptions, disaster recovery, backup procedures, and eDiscovery/audit responses.

STEP 4 Build a data map that identifies the content repositories that contain ESI. You can get started by preparing an ESI data map for all of your organization's electronic records. An ESI data map is a written overview or map of ESI that may, among other things, be used by the legal department in connection with eDiscovery efforts.[18] It typically includes: likely custodians of relevant electronic materials; relevant electronic systems, with scope, character, organization, and formats employed in each system, and any limitations of accessibility; the name of the individuals responsible for electronic document retention policies; and a description of the retention policies for these systems.

A good data map does two things. First, it allows organizations to more quickly locate relevant ESI. Often overlooked, but equally important, a good ESI data map also details and makes an argument for data which isn't reasonably accessible. Walking into a meeting with opposing counsel with a good data map allows you to be much more proactive in limiting the scope of the discovery:

> *"We don't need to conduct discovery activities in our remote offices because they don't have any documents relevant to your request."*

If you can cut the scope of discovery back by 20%, 30%, or more, that translates into real and often significant savings. Clearly, creating an ESI survey data map requires close cooperation between legal, IT and the business; typically, map creation is a joint project. Sometimes, IT has this information readily available an,d other times, storage systems must be surveyed so that the ESI can be classified and captured within the map.

STEP 5 Educate your user community. Without education, policy is meaningless. Continued education is essential in all areas, including changing regulations and changing technologies.

STEP 6 Monitor and measure results. Auditing is key. Data governance is largely about organizational behavior. Organizations change every day and, therefore, their data, its value, and risks also shift rapidly. Unfortunately, most organizations assess themselves only infrequently, if at all. If a business isn't able to change organizational controls to meet demands on a daily or

---

[18] Association for Information and Image Management, "Where is your electronically stored data? Map it," http://www.aiim.org/Infonomics/Electronically-Stored-Data-ROI-2009.aspx, (accessed 1 December 2009).

weekly basis, it isn't governing change. To manage risks, you need to monitor data usage and help ensure effective governance by putting in place a consistent method of documenting organizational best practices and technology that supports the human decision-making process. Monitor how well the organization is performing in the areas of personal data management, email management, content management, application data management, storage management, and retention management. Monitor policies and practices that were put in place to achieve the strategic goals for IG. Make sure you have metrics to measure against.

STEP 7 Establish a continuous improvement process. This should be a living document that's regularly checked for changes in the law, business practices, and so on. You should plan for continuous checkpoints along the way to monitor your governance status, and to allow for remediation and continued education.

Getting Started

The most important step is simply to get started. Looking at the sheer volume of your information and its current state, you may feel that it's impossible to get your arms around this issue. However, the longer you wait, the more difficult it becomes. Choose the areas of highest risk and greatest returns, get them done, and go forward from there.

I once visited a company where the executives lamented their state of disorganization with regard to IG. They told me they were a 150-year-old company with warehouses full of paper records that they couldn't identify, many divisions with disparate systems for electronic records, many years' worth of backup tapes, and other horrors. They stated that they didn't know how to get started and where to begin. They were paralyzed by the scope of their problem. I told them that if they didn't get started, then in five years they would be a 155-year-old company with an even greater mess. Paralysis isn't the answer. Start! You may find that you like the results.

The Mandate is Clear: Gain Control over Information

Sweeping changes across numerous industries have occurred with such force that many organizations and IT departments find themselves insufficiently prepared to respond. One area of change is the multiple regulatory and legislative requirements such as SEC, FINRA, HIPAA, SOX, and the amended FRCP that require tighter control over and governance of corporate information.

How do you deal with this bevy of requirements? The list of hurdles can be just as daunting as finding the right solution. Many of these challenges require you to take a hard look at current business processes and consider a few questions:

- How do you deal with ever-growing volumes of information?

- Is there a better way to manage risk to protect your organization from the threat of unauthorized access to, loss of, or destruction of valuable information assets?

- Can one solution protect and manage information throughout its life cycle while enabling policy and process controls to be applied consistently across content repositories?

- How do you effectively and efficiently search your wealth of content to enable document production for discovery and audit at the lowest cost and with minimal business disruption?

- What processes can you automate to increase usability, minimize administrative tasks, and facilitate compliance?

- Is there a way to improve your retention management practices and ensure that they're consistently followed enterprise-wide for all types of information (physical, electronic, and email)?

As organizations face these issues, they often find that the most pressing requirements begin with email and then continue to all forms of electronic and physical content. But regardless of content type, the message is clear: a comprehensive IG strategy is the key to effectively managing, controlling, securing, and discovering information across the enterprise. Further, as new technologies are rolled out, a comprehensive IG strategy can help you avert potential problems in the future.

Conclusion

Businesses today are faced with new demands that further strain IT departments and affect information strategies. Faced with these pressures, organizations can no longer wait to take steps to gain control. Information is growing exponentially, and eDiscovery and privacy have become major issues. Simultaneously, records management and mainstream compliance efforts must now incorporate physical, electronic, and email management tasks with equal diligence and complete integration. The right solution is one that can unify technologies and simplify processes while meeting these challenges with the least impact to users and at the lowest possible cost of ownership.

Governance and Sustainability

by Steve Boston

The worlds of management and IT are filled with unlikely terms that come to embody a particular subject matter. Such is the case with the word *sustainability*. According to the 1987 Report of the World Commission on Environment and Development, *sustainability* means "meeting the needs of the present without compromising the ability of future generations to meet their own needs."[1] This chapter is all about the idea of sustainability, which

---

[1] United Nations, "Report of the World Commission on Environment and Development", 11 December 1987, http:/www./un.org/documents/ga/res/42/ares42-187.htm (accessed 1 December 2009).

means sustaining your resources, both natural and human, and how an organization can benefit by reconsidering its processes to maximize profits, reduce costs, and minimize its environmental imprint.

Recent corporate focus on sustainability has gotten pretty intense. Still, few companies have formal sustainability programs, let alone chief sustainability officers. The companies that do have them make up a good portion of the Fortune 1000 organizations. Most of those corporations have identified the benefits and risks of sustainability and have the resources to apply to it. Many are now trying to figure out the best way of measuring and managing their programs.

At CA, we created a position that is responsible for developing the company's worldwide strategies and programs for sustainability. Being new to a formalized sustainability position—it isn't something you find on many IT- and developer-based resumes—our first issue was to figure out exactly what *sustainability* means. We found this exercise to be incredibly helpful. It enabled us to speak with a lot of experts and develop our sustainability strategy in a way that made sense for us. It provided us with clear direction on how to proceed to build a sustainability program from the ground up. We now have a strategy in place. We created the Office of Sustainability and developed technology to support our efforts. We formed important relationships within our own industry as well as across other industries, government, and academia.

This has been an intriguing journey of discovery and introspection for us. I sometimes joke that it turns out that saving the planet and all humankind is *way* more difficult than I originally thought it would be.

Somewhere along this journey, it struck me that from a purely business viewpoint, sustainability of and by itself isn't completely sustainable unless you develop it within a business context. Environmentalism can't be sustainable unless you pair it with the economics of the organization.

We've done a lot of thinking about sustainability, and we've realized that much of the drive for environmental and social focus comes from non-business groups—government groups, NGOs, and citizen groups. I think that one of the reasons sustainability programs within an organization have a tough time getting off the ground is because, at first glance, it appears that businesses are being asked to do something that seems to make no business sense. On the surface, sustainability appears to consist of investments of resources that will bear zero return. This is certainly not how business people have been trained to operate! However, upon deeper examination, I've found that if we divide big issues like climate change into pieces that are directly relevant to our businesses and core competencies, we can then frame these investments in a business-positive manner. For this reason, we developed a systematic approach to governing sustainability. (See the section "Building a Sustainability Program" later in this chapter.)

Sustainability Alignment Factors

Our governance approach starts with *sustainability alignment factors*. These are business objectives that an organization strives to achieve through its sustainability initiatives. Suitable factors vary from business to business according to their unique objectives. Focusing attention and metrics around critical alignment factors helps businesses get their heads around how they respond to the pressure to be more sustainable.

Organizations need to arrive at sustainability alignment factors that are meaningful within their industry and then determine how they are going to measure these sustainability alignment factors. Plenty of data, ideas, and opinions exist to start the formulations. But rather than getting hung up on what you don't know, focus on what you *do* know, and demonstrate the ways you're going to use the factors to measure the success of your sustainability programs. Trust me—with the never-ending emergence of new science and the parade of new regulations, you'll have plenty of opportunity down the road to revise these factors.

Potentially, hundreds of factors could be important to different types of organizations. To determine the sustainability alignment factors for *your* organization, ask questions such as these:

- What are the overall objectives of your sustainability program?

- For each objective, who are the stakeholders (employees, customers, board members, company executives, index funds, regulatory bodies, auditors)?

- What are the priorities for each objective?

- What are the specific measurable targets for each objective?

- How do you measure those targets, and how often?

- How do you report on those targets, and how often?

At CA, we chose the following four factors for alignment:

- *Consumption reduction* is designed to help minimize the company's use of natural resources, which in turn can lower its carbon footprint. It involves initiatives such as real estate consolidation, reduced load and timed lighting, print-on-demand printers, and efficient data-center energy management.

- *Cost savings* can be achieved through the judicious application of capital expenditure to projects whose intent is to reduce consumption immediately and produce savings over, say, a three- to ten-year period. It's vital, from a business perspective that consumption-reduction undertakings pay for themselves.

- *Brand enhancement* is an alignment factor that is a Return on Marketing Investment (ROMI) whose effectiveness can be measured in increased sales and unique metrics such as changes in brand perception and customer loyalty. You can determine the latter through periodic surveys. Public demonstration of a company's sustainability strengths may take several forms. They may be as indirect as reporting carbon footprint and energy management numbers in 10-K filings and corporate social responsibility reports, or as direct as a compelling marketing message. GE's Ecomagination campaign is a good example of the latter. You must take special care here to avoid the dreaded *greenwashing*—the practice of making disingenuous claims about your products and policies to make them seem environmentally friendly.

- *Revenue generation* is a fundamental motive of most companies. The ability to generate sustainability-based revenue diverges widely and tends to be based on the sector in which your business participates. CA is one of the world's largest IT management software providers. Our software and expertise was developed to help simplify complex IT environments. CA is fortunate in this regard because our products are designed to help measure, manage, and automate systems, networks, and applications, among other governance roles. CA developed a line of products called ecoSoftware intended to help organizations reduce energy use, cut costs, manage carbon, and become more sustainable. Such software can have a direct impact on the sustainable nature of a business, from metering energy usage to enforcing energy management policies, to governing your overall sustainability program.

Is brand enhancement more important that cost savings? If your answer is "No," then how much more important is cost savings than brand enhancement? Who determines that weighting? This depends a lot on your stakeholders and executive management.

CA's ecoSoftware technology provides an analysis model that allows organizations to define how each of the alignment factors is weighed against the others. This enables organizations to push data from sustainability projects into the model to score them across those alignment factors and in relation to other projects.

The model identifies the potential sustainability success quotient of projects. When you plug in data about specific opportunities, the model helps show you which opportunities you may want to invest in, based on your alignment factors. This can be an efficient way of approaching which sustainability initiatives to tackle, because it helps take out emotional factors and supports fact-based decision making. It forces you to think through why you're doing what you're doing, and what you're hoping to achieve from doing it. It helps build the bridge between business value and social/environmental value in a repeatable way. This is a key to governing sustainability well.

Alignment factors are different for each company and are weighted based on the company's sustainability goals and, ideally, the overall goals of the company. For instance, companies in some industries may desire to focus strongly on brand enhancement, so much of what the company does around sustainability revolves around communicating how it's being a good steward of the environment.

In the retail sector, a company may use increase in market share as a primary alignment factor. It may have a sustainability program dealing directly with consumers, in hopes of increasing market share as a result of its positioning around sustainability. Companies that rely heavily on venture capital may have funding growth as an alignment factor, with the hope of improving their financial investment positions because of their views on the planet and society.

Developing goals, identifying stakeholders, and measuring progress through alignment factors are all critical to governing sustainability.

Investing in Sustainability

Many sustainability projects require an up-front investment of some sort. For the most part, these aren't huge investments. However, when we're going through an economic recession, and when companies are worried about what their revenue streams will look like over the next year or so, it's often hard to begin spending money on sustainability initiatives, especially if companies aren't feeling pressure to invest right now. This is certainly a realistic position that you have to consider. But in my opinion, it's a bit short-sighted.

Some U.S. companies aren't thinking about sustainability just yet because they don't know how it's going to affect them. From a governance perspective, this is risky, given the uncertainty about regulations that may come from the federal government and how those regulations will be worded. How much time will companies have to comply before incurring penalties or lost opportunities? How much reaction time will businesses have prior to a formal carbon trading capability and a formal penalty system for noncompliance? How ready are you to comply with new regulations? Can you differentiate from your competition by getting prepared now? Many feel that regulations are coming and that carbon trading is coming. And those will affect, in a critical manner, the way all business is done.

Organizations with limited resources may be faced with having to prioritize the implementation of their sustainability projects. A well-implemented governance process—and technology to support the process—can help you do the analysis needed to decide where to focus your efforts. It can help you measure costs, risks, and gains against alignment factors to help you determine where to begin. So how do you get started?

Building a Sustainability Program

Define Strategy

The governance vision around sustainability is to provide companies with a systematic life cycle to help them achieve their sustainability goals. CA's ecoSoftware solution provides organizations with technology intended to help enable this governance process for sustainability. It supports a life cycle approach that focuses on continuous improvement and can help organizations with the following areas, as they relate to environmental sustainability:

- Strategy

- Risk management

- Compliance management

- Idea management

- Portfolio management

- Project management

- Performance management and stakeholder reporting

Strategy: For your corporation to successfully govern its sustainability programs, you must first define your sustainability strategy. What are the company's key objectives? What are the sustainability alignment factors? What policies must be put in place to promote the right behavior? What are the Key Performance Indicators (KPIs) that align with those objectives?

Risk Management: After you've defined your sustainability strategy, you should look at the risks you face in meeting the objectives of that strategy. You can also look at your company's environmental risks of not putting a strategy in place. Understanding these risks and putting in place action plans and initiatives to mitigate those risks will help you achieve your objectives.

Compliance Management: Many companies today are faced with environmental legislation with which they need to comply. Additionally, Europe and Australia have put in place cap-and-trade systems for carbon, and similar federal legislation have been discussed in the U.S. To effectively govern compliance, you must encapsulate applicable regulations in a central repository, design appropriate policies, and quantify progress toward fulfillment. This can include capturing overall energy consumption, emissions from operations, and the net affect these have on your organization's overall carbon footprint.

Idea Management: Obtaining input from internal and external stakeholders provides companies with a large pool of ideas to consider and assess, from operational improvements in your business processes, to new product ideas, to improvements up and down your supply chain. Being able to capture, categorize, inventory, and perform an initial evaluation of these ideas can enable you to better manage your portfolio of investments.

Portfolio Management: The reality is that demand typically exceeds available capacity; therefore, only some of the presented ideas can ever be formally evaluated. It's important to understand the financial ROI of the proposed initiatives, but it's also vital to take into account other aspects of these initiatives. For example:

- How well does the initiative align to the company's overall sustainability objectives and goals?

- Will this initiative reduce your energy consumption and, in turn, overall carbon footprint? If so, by how much?

- What is the impact on your brand image of implementing this initiative (or not)?

- Who are the key internal and external stakeholders that have a vested interest in this initiative?

You need to take a comprehensive view of your company's initiatives to ensure that you're investing in projects that will give you the most return from an overall sustainability alignment factor perspective.

Project Management: The initiatives you identify need to be managed effectively. Resources need to be assigned, milestones set, time and cost tracked. The project's results must be monitored as it progresses, and compared to the expected return.

Performance Management and Stakeholder Reporting: Measurement is an important aspect of performance management. You need to track your progress against your stated goals and objectives. Capturing and analyzing environmental activity data such as energy consumption, energy spend, and the associated carbon footprint metrics are becoming increasingly important to organizations. Bringing this information together in a central repository makes it easier to report to stakeholders.

Build the Program

How do you build a sustainability program? First and foremost, you must figure out what your goals are. Why is sustainability important to your company? Different companies have different sustainability goals. Some have multiple goals; others have only one or two. For instance, perhaps managing your carbon footprint is important to your company. Some companies may care more about brand enhancement. Others may focus on community relations. Every industry places different levels of importance on different factors.

We decided that the function of sustainability at CA is to develop the programs and strategies that are necessary to protect, nurture, and grow all the resources we need to remain a viable business into the future. We categorize these resources into the following three groups:

Environmental resource group: Things like breathable air, drinkable water, electrical power for our data centers, and heat in our buildings. Losing any of these environmentally based resources could have a negative impact on our business.

Community-based resources: Resources that are all about people. If we don't have people to build our products, people to sell our products, and people to buy our products, our business could be as negatively impacted as if we didn't have clean air to breathe. So, it's very important that we provide a level of care and nurturing for these people and the communities that support them.

Economic resources: Top line, bottom line, fiduciary responsibility, governance, and compliance. Because we're a business, these require special attention. Recently, we've seen a number of examples in the news of what can happen to companies that don't maintain sustainable business and economic models.

At CA, we focus our efforts across all three of these resource groups. As an IT provider, we manage to mix the economic group and the environmental group together. We blend our environmental priorities with our social ones, and feel that providing technology for social benefit in an economically sustainable way is a goal that makes good business sense.

We established the four sustainability alignment objectives mentioned earlier, which we use to determine the success of our sustainability programs. Consumption reduction is an important alignment factor. Specifically, we track our carbon footprint—a great area for measurement because it has a clear starting point. From there, it's easy to track our progress as the carbon footprint demonstrates the effects operations have on carbon and greenhouse gas emissions. We're also beginning to look at other areas including water, waste, and paper.

Our second alignment factor has to do with brand enhancement. We want our customers to know that we care about sustainability, so it's important that we clearly and transparently communicate our positioning.

The third thing we care about is operational cost savings. This is the area in which many companies can easily recognize ROI. A strong relationship exists between the sustainability goal of consumption reduction and economic benefit.

Our vice president of global facilities invited in waste-removal professionals to talk about trash and recycling. In the course of the discussion, we discovered that much of what we order is delivered to our sites on pallets. Each pallet is made of wood and wrapped in plastic.

It became clear to us that we were paying suppliers to ship us all that garbage (they cover their packaging costs in their product price), then paying someone on our staff to break it up, and then paying someone else to pick it up and ship it someplace where it takes up space. We found that we could purchase a bailer so we could bail up the plastic and stack the pallets. Then, we could arrange for other people to come and take this stuff away for recycling. This is amazing! We eliminated much of the costs of the waste disposal; and every time someone comes to pick up the bails, they hand us a check. Needless to say, the bailer paid for itself in no time. There are all kinds of examples like this that show the very close association between cost avoidance and carbon and waste reduction.

The fourth and final alignment factor (or measurement) we chose for CA is revenue. In terms of economic resources, we can't ignore that. We're a business. We exist to provide ongoing financial value to our shareholders. It's what helps fuel our ability to make a difference. *And* it's a fantastic way of proving to ourselves our focus on sustainability has value. Every dollar of revenue or dollar saved from operations represents helping the environmental resources of the planet.

Some companies may not have a revenue opportunity associated with sustainability. But those that do must answer this question: How can you map your core competencies toward a service or product that will help your customers support their own sustainability efforts? In the case of CA, we're a leading providers of enterprise IT management products. We've been helping to unify IT operations for years. Now, with our ecoSoftware products, we're expanding that base to include management from energy, carbon, and sustainability perspectives. In addition, we're working with the World Economic Forum to help figure out how IT competencies can be applied in new ways, outside of traditional IT boundaries, to help solve some of the problems facing the world today. Because we're a business, we deliver these innovations to our customers via our product offerings, and this helps us produce revenue.

It's interesting to note that this revenue-producing model is an underlying force that helps ensure the development of solutions that support sustainability. These solutions aren't dependent on friendly politics or small groups of people who want change; they exist because of their ability to generate profits. For this reason, I feel that at the end of the day, businesses will play an important role in helping to solve sustainability problems because they're incented to look for profitable solutions. When it comes to the development and maintenance of long-term, sustainable solutions to these problems, profit is an important motivator.

Align Support

Sustainability from an organizational support perspective can be easier than many other programs you've kicked off, not to mention that you'll get to play instant hero.

Define your alignment factors, and then define a project around sustainability—a relatively easy task. Such a process can help relieve some of the pressure your company is experiencing. Executives in many businesses are experiencing pressure from their customers, their families, their Boards of Directors, and their employees to be more sustainable. After you define your sustainability program, is it easier to receive immediate executive support.

Gaining colleague and employee support can be easier as well. When you're implementing a sustainability program, everybody wants to help. Everyone wants to help save the planet. Everyone wants to work for companies that do that. At CA, the amount of support the Office of Sustainability has gotten from above, below, and sideways has been overwhelming and timely.

Select a Starting Point

A good place for an organization to embark on its sustainability initiative is by determining its carbon footprint. Begin by measuring your carbon footprint from an internal operations perspective. You need to examine a number of categories. For example, look at the carbon footprint of your real estate portfolio and your energy and gas consumption. Look at food service operations. Look at procurement. Look at IT operations.

According to the U.S. Environmental Protection Agency (EPA) Climate Change website (http://www.epa.gov/climatechange), the term *carbon footprint* describes the amount of greenhouse gases (GHG) that are emitted into the atmosphere each year by an entity such as a person, a household, a building, an organization, or a company. It's usually measured in units of carbon dioxide equivalents.

The EPA goes on to say the following:

> *"A carbon footprint usually includes both direct and indirect GHG emissions:*
>
> - *Direct emissions are considered to be emissions that are directly under the control of the person or company. For example, when a person drives his or her car it emits GHGs. For a company, if it chooses to heat its factory by burning a fuel, those are direct emissions.*
>
> - *Indirect emissions are emissions that are a consequence of the activities of the reporting entity, but that occur at sources owned or controlled by another entity. For example, purchased electricity is considered an indirect emission. While a person or company can control the amount of electricity that is purchased, they cannot control the emissions that are associated with the generation of that electricity. Those emissions are under the direct control of someone else. For example, a person with a small carbon footprint would engage in activities that limit the amount of GHGs he or she emits in the course of a year. Carbon dioxide is the primary GHG emitted in*

industrialized countries, and emissions of other GHGs are often expressed in terms of their equivalent value in carbon or carbon dioxide. A person's carbon footprint would include all the GHG emissions associated with his or her activities, not just those of carbon dioxide."[2]

Organizations looking to gain an in-depth understanding of the factors that contribute to their overall carbon footprint should consult The Greenhouse Gas Protocol®. According to that document, "The Greenhouse Gas Protocol (GHG Protocol) is the most widely used international accounting tool for government and business leaders to understand, quantify, and manage greenhouse gas emissions. The GHG Protocol® Initiative, a decade-long partnership between the World Resources Institute and the World Business Council for Sustainable Development, is working with businesses, governments, and environmental groups around the world to build a new generation of credible and effective emissions accounting and reduction programs for tackling climate change."[3]

The GHG Protocol Corporate Accounting and Reporting Standard provides a step-by-step guide for companies to use in quantifying and reporting their GHG emissions. It's available at the GHG Protocol Initiative website (ghgprotocol.org) and is a useful resource for corporations looking to govern sustainability.

---

[2] U.S. Environmental Protection Agency, Climate Change Frequent Questions, http://climatechange.custhelp.com/cgi-bin/climatechange.cfg/php/enduser/std_adp.php?p_faqid=5401 (accessed 1 December 2009).

[3] The Greenhouse Gas Protocol Initiative, http://www.ghgprotocol.org (accessed 1 December 2009).

According to the GHG Protocol, companies calculate their GHG emissions using the following steps:

1. *Identify GHG emissions sources.* Some sources are fuels in heating systems, fuels in transportation devices such as automobiles, and emissions from physical or chemical processes.

2. *Select a GHG emissions calculation approach.* The most common approach is through the application of emission factors that relate emissions sources to carbon. Emission factors differ according to a multitude of variables including geographic region.

3. *Collect activity data, and choose emission factors.* Typical activity data includes amount of fuel purchased, amount of metered electricity consumed, and number of passenger miles traveled. Emission factors are available to translate that activity data into GHG emissions. These factors differ according to a wide range of variables including geographic region and degree of specificity. For example, the number of kilowatt hours (kWh) consumed, multiplied by an emission factor of 1.5 pounds, yields the number of pounds of carbon produced.

4. *Apply calculation tools.* Tools are available that range from simplistic and generic to highly sophisticated and customized by industry.

5. *Roll up GHG emissions data to a corporate level.* As you've seen throughout this book, centralizing information at the corporate level helps ensure consistency and good governance.[4]

In addition to reporting on absolute amounts of carbon dioxide-equivalent emissions, it's important to look at the organization's emissions in relation to other business-relevant metrics called *intensity metrics*. Intensity metrics tie emissions to business-relevant metrics such as sales, revenues, office

---

[4] The Greenhouse Gas Protocol Initiative, "A Corporate Accounting and Reporting Standard", http://www.ghgprotocol.org/standards/corporate-standard (accessed 1 December 2009).

space, and numbers of employees. Tracking emissions by intensity provides a relative measure of emissions that is more meaningful, because emissions are put in the context of the state of the business. For example, if the reduction of an organization's annual emissions is due to a divestiture, then theoretically, annual emissions per revenue dollar may stay the same or, worse, may increase. Conversely, a rise in annual emissions tracked to adding a new manufacturing plant should not necessarily be viewed negatively, because the rest of the organization may have made significant strides in being more efficient in their energy use for the existing portfolio of plants. If the organization only looked at reporting in absolute terms, they would see an increase. However, when looking at an intensity metric that takes into account the overall square footage of the portfolio, annual emissions per square foot would show a decrease when compared to the prior year, and as such would make for a more meaningful comparison.

CA selects sustainability projects in part based on the probability of a reasonable time to value. That's probably true for most companies, although I wouldn't suggest that it's absolutely true for every company. For example, if a company's only alignment factor is brand enhancement, it's possible that the company may view its sustainability initiative as a loss leader.

Some companies may be missing opportunities around sustainability because of the immaturity of their governance process. It requires a little thinking out of the box. Think about your surroundings, your places of business, where you ship from, and where you're shipping to. Where is the waste? What can be done about it? Who may benefit from by-products of your business? What can you do for your community, and what can it do for you? What can your suppliers do, and what can you do for them? Are their processes as automated as possible? What can you learn from them? How about your competition? What are other businesses outside your domain doing?

You may be able to consolidate office space. Maybe you can install solar panels in the parking lots and on the roof tops. You can do all kinds of things; but when you look at those opportunities, you must be able to go back and measure the cost of doing them specific to your company's sustainability alignment factors (cost savings or consumption reduction, for example). Remember, sustainability for business isn't philanthropic; it's designed to solve very specific problems while clearly delivering shareholder value.

You need to look at everything you're doing and examine it from every angle to ensure that it's a good business opportunity before you invest money in it. Without having your sustainability programs connected to the rest of the business, the answers you get in terms of ROI and business management may not be the correct answers when observed from much broader viewpoints.

Practice Good Governance

Build well-designed governance into your sustainability initiative from the start. This is key. Integrate your governance around sustainability with the rest of the company's governance methods. Keep an eye on regulatory requirements and their effect on your company.

One of the underlying issues you have to figure out is how to govern in a way that doesn't create an incredible amount of overhead. On one hand, being able to collect data, measure data, baseline data, report on data, and organize data is increasingly useful from many different perspectives. On the other hand, if you're spending 90% of your resources plugging data into those applications, then your cost is too heavy. You need to automate data collection in an optimal manner so that you don't expend valuable resources just entering data or reporting on progress. You also need to analyze opportunities and inspect the ROI across sustainability projects. In general, green initiatives should save you money or make you money. They shouldn't cost you money.

Carbon Trading Is Coming

All companies need to pay attention to issues related to carbon. Carbon trading/taxation and carbon penalties are coming and may already be in place when you read this. Dealing with these new issues will require a great deal of governance.

As of July 2009, the proposed American Clean Energy and Security Act of 2009[5] (H.R. 2454) would establish an economy-wide cap-and-trade program and create other incentives and standards for increasing energy efficiency and low-carbon energy consumption.

According to the EPA website, "cap and trade is a market-based policy tool for protecting human health and the environment by controlling large amounts of emissions from a group of sources. A cap and trade program first sets an aggressive cap, or maximum limit, on emissions. Sources covered by the program then receive authorizations to emit in the form of emissions allowances, with the total amount of allowances limited by the cap. Each source can design its own compliance strategy to meet the overall reduction requirement, including the sale or purchase of allowances, installation of pollution controls, and implementation of efficiency measures, among other options. Individual control requirements are not specified under a cap and trade program, but each emission source must surrender allowances equal to its actual emissions in order to comply. Sources must also completely and accurately measure and report all emissions in a timely manner to guarantee that the overall cap is achieved."[6]

SO WHAT'S THE BIG DEAL?

by Terrence G. Clark, SVP and GM, CA ecoSoftware
The IT Greenability Blog, 23 April 2009,
community.ca.com/blogs/greenit

Reading the news every day, it appears the United States keeps moving one step closer to some form of mandatory greenhouse gas regulation.

Last week, the EPA issued a proposed finding that greenhouse gases are contributors of air pollution, which in turn endangers the public

---

[5] The Library of Congress, H.R. 2454 American Clean Energy and Security Act of 2009, http://thomas.loc.gov/cgi-bin/query/z?c111:H.R.2454: (accessed 1 December 2009).

[6] Environmental Protection Agency, "Cap and Trade: Basic Information," http://www.epa.gov/captrade/basic-info.html, 3 December 2009.

health and welfare. When I asked an associate of mine what he thought about this announcement, he said, "So what's the big deal? I could have told you that without having to perform a major study."

To understand why it is a big deal, you really have to go back to 1963, when the U.S. passed the original Clean Air Act of 1963 to clean up air pollution. That act merely instituted a fund to perform a study on air pollution and to pay for some of the cleanup efforts.

Then, in 1970, came a stronger Clean Air Act and the creation of the EPA. The EPA's primary role was to carry out the law to ensure the reduction of air pollution across the United States.

However over the years, it was difficult for the EPA to penalize a company that was in violation of the Clean Air Act. The agency had to go to court for every little thing, which certainly wasn't a viable option that would scale. Then, in 1990, new amendments to the Act strengthened the EPA's power to include civil and criminal sanctions, including financial penalties.

In 2007, the Supreme Court ordered a scientific review of the effects of greenhouse gases. The EPA's proposed finding last week was the output of that order.

Given the EPA's charter and ability to put in place sanctions and financial penalties as it sees fit to reduce air pollution, it's now in a very interesting position. The EPA could decide to put in place any type of regulation it felt was necessary to address the problem, and it wouldn't need congressional approval to do so. If this were to happen, depending on how strict the regulation was, it could have a very significant impact on organizations around the country.

As it stands now, the EPA has indicated that it would prefer to see comprehensive legislation put in place to deal with air pollution. However, if that gets stalled in Congress, don't be surprised to see the EPA act.

Many high-emitting corporations fear the unknown, which is why they are promoting legislation. That way, they can at least have a chance to help shape it.

One thing looks to be for sure: carbon regulation in the U.S. *is coming* and will have an effect on many organizations. To my associate who asked the question—that, my friend, is the big deal.

At this point, the U.S.'s legislative branch of government is focused on those companies that produce the most pollution, which in effect means they emit the most carbon dioxide into the atmosphere. As a result, those companies involved with manufacturing, mining, oil drilling, and refining may be more affected initially, but this impact will expand to other industries. The number of small and medium companies that may be able to accomplish some level of carbon reduction probably match or outweigh the relatively small number of companies in the U.S. that manufacture or drill for oil.

One of the problems associated with carbon trading is that the amount of governance overhead required increases dramatically due to strict guidelines and oversight that are needed to calculate, track, and verify emissions as well as an organization's carbon credits.

If you go back to when emissions testing of vehicles started, around the mid to late 1970s, it closely followed the gasoline shortage. It's evident that emissions testing had as much or more to do with gasoline usage than it had to do with pollution. We're seeing something similar today: solar technology companies made great progress while the cost of crude was high; but as prices subside, there is less investment in these companies and less interest in them from venture capitalists. However, the current administration is pushing for incentives to maintain and increase investments in these new technologies that reduce our dependency on fossil fuels.

National carbon footprint reduction can't be done on an industry-by-industry basis. Here's the reason why. One of the things you have to understand about alternative energies is that right now, an incredible amount of money revolves around oil. An entire economic system is built around oil. If the U.S. wants to reduce the dependency on oil, not only do we have to create alternative sources of energy, but we also have to figure out how to move away from the oil economy.

Follow the money. If we don't replace the economy around oil, it doesn't matter how many alternatives we come up with, we're not likely to reduce U.S. dependency on oil. If we're going to move the economy off oil to alternative sources, then we'll have to treat all industries and all business similarly from a regulatory perspective. We can't have different benchmarks and different goals for different industries. We have to be able to say carbon is worth X amount of money. And then it has to be worth X regardless of the country, currency, or industry. People understand dollars, euros, or whatever currency is used, so establishing a reasonable valuation standard is key.

Manufacturing companies can potentially make incredible amounts of money from carbon trading. The trick that makes this work is that the money the big manufacturing companies make off carbon trading must be immediately reinvested to retool the way they do business. Their cost to reduce carbon is significantly higher than the cost would be for the local country store. So, it plays out acceptably at the end if we have a standardized set of metrics for determining the saleable carbon and the associated price of that carbon.

To be successful, carbon trading must be accompanied by strict guidelines (regulations) and high penalties so that we keep the number of gamers (people and organizations trying to beat the system) relatively low. If the U.S. does this right, we'll create a system that can hopefully absorb 5–10% anomalies relatively easily.

But we must watch out for derivatives games. We just saw how this played out in the mortgage business. Generally speaking, derivatives were a relatively new game that hadn't been applied at this scale before. Our eyes have been opened. Risk remains risk, regardless of how it's spread.

IT and Sustainability

As stated earlier, one of CA's sustainability alignment factors is revenue generation. Accordingly, one aspect of CA's sustainability program focuses on taking what we've learned about sustainability, mapping that to our IT management core competencies, and figuring out how we can best help our customers become more sustainable.

IT consumes about 1.5% of the generation capacity of the U.S. The EPA projects that this percentage will rise as data center consumption needs outpace the country's generation capacity. If state-of-the-art efficiencies and operations within the data center are employed, IT consumption may peak at 2–4% in the near term.[7]

Approaching sustainability from an IT management perspective can allow us to manage sustainability in real time. We can move work around, and we can do all kinds of interesting things to make automated, ongoing, constant improvements in energy cost, consumption, and associated carbon factors. It's amazing when you realize how this can play out.

Conclusion

Let's face it. From a sustainability viewpoint, we've got some big problems in the world. I believe they're solvable if all businesses take a good governance approach to sustainability. Businesses can develop healthy profit models, and together we can help eradicate some environmental and social issues while doing so. We need to tie all the governance related to sustainability back into the integration points across the rest of the business.

Businesses understand that there are some real issues here. We understand that business is a major contributor to those issues—and we understand money can be saved and money can be made by tackling those issues.

Among the citizenry, government, and business, I believe business can have a major impact on reducing environmental and social issues. We in business have to make sure we don't get confused by the hype or the fear. We need to figure out how to reset the world, reset business, and work with government *and* the citizenry in a concise, planned, and coordinated way to help reduce global pollution. This is far bigger than just reducing the use of plastic cups.

---

[7] U.S. Environmental Protection Agency, "Report to Congress on Server and Data Center Energy Efficiency", Public Law 109-431, http://www.energystar.gov/ia/partners/prod_development/downloads/EPA_Datacent er_Report_Congress_Final1.pdf (accessed 1 December 2009).

When we look at the resources we have to manage, a pure business need exists for measurement. We have to ask ourselves a lot of questions. What is our sustainability strategy? How well are we executing against that strategy? Does the strategy make sense? Is it providing us with the returns we forecast? How do we report on the relative success or failure of components of our sustainability strategy—and who cares about that kind of reporting? These kinds of questions are important not just for our own management but also for our customers, partners, security indexes, and, soon, government.

More and more, we get requests for disclosure of CA's sustainability status. I think this is good news in that it's an indicator that companies are becoming more aware of the need for sustainability, auditing, and sustainability reporting. That leads me to believe that business is on the road to helping to fix some of the most pervasive issues facing mankind today. This is great news.

Corporate Governance Principles of CA, Inc.

General

These Corporate Governance Principles (these "Principles") have been approved by the Board of Directors of CA, Inc. (the "Company") and provide the basic outline of the Company's corporate governance.

Role and Functions of the Board

The Board is elected by the stockholders to oversee the business and affairs of the Company, to oversee management, to build long-term value for the stockholders, and to sustain the Company's vitality for its stockholders and other constituencies, including its employees.

In addition to these general roles, the Board performs a number of more specific functions, including:

- Selecting and overseeing the evaluation of the Chief Executive Officer (the "CEO");

- Overseeing CEO and senior management succession planning;

- Providing counsel and oversight on the selection, evaluation and development of senior management;

- Reviewing and approving corporate strategy on an annual basis;

- Advising and counseling the CEO and senior management on relevant topics;

- Reviewing, monitoring and, where appropriate, approving fundamental financial and business strategies and major corporate actions;

- Assessing major risks facing the Company and considering strategies for their management and mitigation; and

- Overseeing and evaluating processes designed to maintain the integrity of the Company, including the integrity of its financial statements, its compliance with law and ethics, and its relationships with its employees, customers, suppliers and other stakeholders.

Director Qualifications

Directors should possess the highest personal and professional ethics, integrity and values, and must be committed to representing the long-term interests of the Company and its stockholders. They must have an inquisitive and objective perspective, practical wisdom and mature judgment, as well as an understanding of the Company's business and the willingness to question what they do not understand.

Each director should be free of any conflict of interest which would interfere with the proper performance of the responsibilities of a director.

Directors must be willing to devote sufficient time to carrying out their duties and responsibilities effectively. To ensure that a director has sufficient time to devote, no director may serve on more than three boards of directors of public companies in addition to the Company's Board.

A director who retires or who has a material change in his or her principal occupation or business association since his or her most recent election to the Board shall tender a resignation from the Board to the Chair of the Corporate Governance Committee. The Board, upon recommendation of the Corporate Governance Committee, shall determine whether to accept the resignation. In addition, to enable the Corporate Governance Committee to monitor compliance with the criteria for service as a director, as well as for service on a particular Board Committee, the Corporate Governance Committee shall be notified promptly of (1) the proposed election of a director to the board of directors (or similar body) or any board committee of another entity (other than not-for-profit entities), (2) a director's removal or other cessation of service as a member of any such board or committee, and (3) any other development that could affect a director's ability to serve on the Board or any Board Committee. The Corporate Governance Committee shall recommend to the Board whether such director should resign or be removed as a director of the Company or as a member of any Board Committee, or whether any other action should be taken.

Director Independence

A majority of the directors must be independent directors, as determined by the Board on the recommendation of the Corporate Governance Committee, based on the guidelines set forth below. The Board believes that the CEO should serve on the Board. At no time shall more than two employees of the Company (including the CEO) serve on the Board; provided, that if the total number of directors exceeds twelve, no more than 25% of the total number of directors may be employees of the Company.

For a director to be considered independent, the Board must determine that the director does not have any relationship which, in the opinion of the Board, would interfere with the exercise of independent judgment in carrying out the responsibilities of a director. The Board has established guidelines to assist it in determining director independence in conformity with The NASDAQ Stock Market LLC ("NASDAQ") listing requirements. In addition, the Board will consider all relevant facts and circumstances in making an independence determination, not only from the standpoint of the director, but also from that of persons or organizations with which the director has an affiliation.

A director will not be independent if:

- The director is, or at any time during the past three years was, employed by the Company (provided that employment by a director as an executive officer on an interim basis for a period no longer than one year will not disqualify that director from being considered independent following such employment);

- A family member of the director is, or at any time during the past three years was, employed by the Company as an executive officer;

- The director or a family member of the director accepted any compensation from the Company in excess of $120,000 during any period of 12 consecutive months within the past three years (provided that compensation received by the director for former service as an executive officer on an interim basis for a period no longer than one year will not be considered in determining independence following such service), other than (i) compensation for Board or Board committee service, (ii) compensation paid to a family member of the director who is an employee (other than an executive officer) of the Company or (iii) benefits under a tax-qualified retirement plan, or non-discretionary compensation;

- The director or a family member of the director is a partner in, or a controlling shareholder or an executive officer of, any organization to which the Company made, or from which the Company received payments for property or services in the current or any of the past three fiscal years that exceed 2% of the recipient's consolidated gross revenues for that year or $200,000, whichever is more, other than (i) payments arising solely from investments in the Company's securities or (ii) payments under non-discretionary charitable contribution matching programs;

- The director or a family member of the director is an executive officer of another entity where at any time during the past three years any of the executive officers of the Company served on the compensation committee of such other entity; or

- The director or a family member of the director is a current partner or employee of the Company's outside auditor, or was a partner or an employee of the Company's outside auditor who worked on the Company's audit at any time during any of the past three years.

Any one or more of the following relationships, whether individually or in any combination, will be considered immaterial and will not, in and of themselves, impair the director's independence:

Payments To/From the Company

1. The director or a family member of the director is a partner in or an executive officer of another company or entity to which the Company made or from which the Company received payments for property or services in an amount that does not exceed, in the current or any of the past three fiscal years 2% of the recipient's consolidated gross revenues for that year or $200,000, whichever is more, other than (i) payments arising solely from investments in the Company's securities or (ii) payments under non-discretionary charitable contribution matching programs;

2. The director and family members of the director directly or indirectly own, in the aggregate, a 10% or greater equity interest in another company or entity to which the Company made or from which the Company received payments for property or services in an amount that does not exceed, in the current or any of the past three fiscal years 2% of the recipient's consolidated gross revenues for that year or $200,000, whichever is more, other than (i) payments arising solely from investments in the Company's securities or (ii) payments under non-discretionary charitable contribution matching programs;

Indebtedness

1. The director or a family member of the director is a partner in or an executive officer of another company or entity that is indebted to the Company, or to which the Company is indebted, and the total amount of either company's (or entity's) indebtedness to the other at the end of the last completed fiscal year is less than 2% of the other company's or entity's total consolidated assets;

2. The director and family members of the director directly or indirectly own, in the aggregate, a 10% or greater equity interest in another company or entity that is indebted to the Company, or to which the Company is indebted, and the total

amount of either company's (or entity's) indebtedness to the other at the end of the last completed fiscal year is less than 2% of the other company's or entity's total consolidated assets;

Charitable Contributions

1. The director or a family member of the director is an executive officer, of a charitable organization, and the Company's discretionary charitable contributions to the organization (i.e., other than contributions made under the Company's matching grant program) do not exceed, in the current or any of the past three fiscal years, 2% of the charitable organization's consolidated gross revenues for that year or $200,000 whichever is more;

Directorships

1. The director or family member of the director is a director, advisory director or trustee (or serves in a similar position) of another company, entity or charitable organization that engages in any transactions (including indebtedness transactions), or has any other relationships, with the Company (including any contributions by the Company to any such charitable organization);

Less Than 10% Equity Interest

1. The director and the family members of the director directly or indirectly own, in the aggregate, less than a 10% equity interest in another company or entity that engages in any transactions (including indebtedness transactions), or has any other relationships, with the Company;

Other

1. The director or a family member of the director is an employee (but not an executive officer) of another company, entity or charitable organization that engages in any transactions (including indebtedness transactions), or has any other relationships, with the Company (including any contributions by the Company to any such charitable organization);

2. A member of the director's family (other than a family member) serves in any capacity with the Company; or

3. A member of the director's family (other than a family member) serves in any capacity with, or owns any equity interest in, another company, entity or charitable organization that engages in any transactions (including indebtedness transactions), or has any other relationships, with the Company (including any contributions by the Company to any such charitable organization).

Notwithstanding the foregoing, the Board (on the recommendation of the Corporate Governance Committee) may determine that a director who has a relationship that exceeds the limits described in the immediately preceding paragraph (but only to the extent that the Board determines that the director does not have any direct or indirect material relationship with the Company and any such relationship does not constitute a bar to independence under NASDAQ listing requirements) is nonetheless independent.

For purposes of these Principles, the term "family member" means a person's spouse, parents, children, and siblings, whether by blood, marriage or adoption, or anyone residing in such person's home.

The ownership of stock in the Company by directors is encouraged and the ownership of a substantial amount of stock in the Company shall not in itself be a basis for a determination that a director is not independent.

The Board will undertake an annual review of the independence of all non-employee directors, based on the recommendation of the Corporate Governance Committee.

Size of Board

The Corporate Governance Committee considers and makes recommendations to the Board concerning the appropriate size and needs of the Board, taking into account the Board's ability to function effectively and with appropriate diversity and expertise.

The Corporate Governance Committee shall be responsible for selecting and recommending to the Board candidates to fill vacancies on the Board that occur as a result of expansion of the size of the Board, by resignation, by retirement or for any other reason.

Period of Board Service

A non-employee director shall serve until the annual meeting after his or her 75th birthday and for a maximum of ten years; provided, however, that the Board, on the recommendation of the Corporate Governance Committee, may waive such age and/or term limitation if circumstances warrant.

Director Selection Process

All directors shall stand for election by the stockholders each year at the Company's Annual Meeting of Stockholders. The Board, on the recommendation of the Corporate Governance Committee, shall propose a slate of nominees for election at each such meeting. In addition, between such meetings, the Board, on the recommendation of the Corporate Governance Committee, may elect directors to serve until the next such meeting.

Stockholders may propose nominees for consideration by the Corporate Governance Committee in accordance with procedures developed by that Committee and disclosed in the Company's Proxy Statement each year.

Each director shall submit his or her Irrevocable Resignation (as defined below) in writing to the Chairman of the Corporate Governance Committee. The Board shall nominate for re-election as a director only an incumbent candidate who has tendered, prior to the mailing of the proxy statement for the annual meeting at which he or she is to be re-elected as a director, an irrevocable resignation authorized by Section 141(b) of the Delaware General Corporation Law that will be effective upon (i) the failure to receive the required vote at any annual meeting at which such candidate is nominated for re-election and (ii) Board acceptance of such resignation (an "Irrevocable Resignation"). In addition, the Board shall fill director vacancies and new directorships only with candidates who tender, at or prior to the time of their appointment to the Board, the same form of Irrevocable Resignation tendered by other directors in accordance herewith.

The Corporate Governance Committee (or such other committee comprised of independent directors as the Board may appoint) shall consider the Irrevocable Resignation submitted by any director not receiving the requisite number of votes to be elected pursuant to Section 7 of Article II of the Bylaws and shall recommend to the Board the action to be taken with respect to such tendered resignation. If no independent directors received the required majority vote, the Board shall act on the resignation offers. Any director whose Irrevocable Resignation is under consideration pursuant to this provision shall not participate in the committee recommendation regarding whether to accept the resignation offer. The Board shall take action within 90 days following certification of the vote, unless such action would cause the Company to fail to comply with any requirement of NASDAQ or any rule or regulation promulgated under the Securities Exchange Act of 1934, in which event the Company shall take action as promptly as is practicable while continuing to meet such requirements. The Board will promptly disclose its decision and the reasons therefore in a Form

8-K furnished to the Securities and Exchange Commission. After accepting a director's resignation, the Board may fill any resulting vacancy or may decrease the size of the Board.

Former CEOs and Other Employee's Board Membership

The Board believes that the Board membership of the CEO and other employees of the Company following their resignation or retirement from the Company is a matter to be decided in each individual instance. When the CEO no longer holds that position or an employee director resigns or retires as an employee of the Company, resignation from the Board should be offered at the same time.

Meetings

The Board should have at least five scheduled meetings each year. There shall be an agenda for each meeting, focusing on relevant issues for the Board's consideration. Directors are expected to attend all scheduled meetings of the Board and the Committees on which they serve, as well as meetings of the Company's stockholders.

The independent directors will have regularly scheduled meetings at least twice a year at which only independent directors are present. The Chairman of the Board (if he or she is an independent director) or the Lead Independent Director (described below), if any, shall preside at those meetings.

Agendas and other meeting materials should be distributed in advance of Board and Committee meetings so as to provide the directors sufficient time to review such materials; the directors are expected to review such materials. Directors are encouraged to make suggestions as to agenda items and to ask that additional information be provided to the Board or any Committee to facilitate its performance.

On an annual basis, the Secretary of the Company shall prepare and distribute to the directors a detailed calendar of the meetings scheduled to be held by the Board and each of its Committees during the ensuing year. The calendar shall also specify the matters to be considered and acted upon at each such meeting, to the extent known at such time.

Board Leadership

The Board has no policy with respect to separation of the positions of Chairman and CEO or with respect to whether the Chairman should be a member of management or a non-management director, and believes that these are matters that should be discussed and determined by the Board from time to time. When the Chairman of the Board is a member of management or is otherwise not independent, the non-employee directors shall elect annually, on the recommendation of the Corporate Governance Committee, a Lead Independent Director. The duties of the Lead Independent Director (or the Chairman, if he or she is independent) shall include presiding at executive sessions of the non-employee and independent directors.

Board Self-Assessment

The Board shall conduct an annual self-assessment of its performance to determine whether the Board and its Committees are functioning effectively.

Board Compensation

Directors who are employees shall not receive any compensation, directly or indirectly, for their services as directors. The Corporate Governance Committee shall be responsible for recommending to the Board the compensation and any benefits for non-employee directors, which shall be subject to the full discussion and approval by the Board. In discharging this duty, the Corporate Governance Committee shall be guided by three goals: (1) compensation should fairly pay directors for the work they perform; (2) compensation should include a significant equity component to align directors' interests with the long-term interests of stockholders; and (3) the structure of the compensation should be simple, transparent and easy for stockholders to understand.

Stock Ownership Guideline for Non-Employee Directors

Consistent with our director compensation programs, each non-employee director receives at least 50% of his or her director compensation in the form of equity in the Company, which may not be transferred until after the director's retirement.

Counsel and Other Advisors; Company Funding Obligations

The Board shall have the authority, to the extent deemed necessary or appropriate, to retain and terminate independent legal counsel or other advisors to assist the Board in carrying out its responsibilities. The Company shall provide for appropriate funding, as determined by the Board, to pay any such counsel or other advisors retained by the Board.

Access to Management and Outside Counsel and Auditors

Non-employee directors may contact senior managers of the Company and the Company's outside counsel and auditors without the permission of senior corporate management, and without such management being present. To facilitate such contact, non-employee directors are encouraged to periodically visit Company locations without senior corporate management being present.

Director Orientation and Education

The Company shall provide orientation for new directors. Such orientation shall include information concerning the Company's business and operations, as well as its corporate governance and other relevant matters, and shall be coordinated by the Secretary, under the guidance of the Corporate Governance Committee.

The Company shall also provide continuing education for directors, which may include programs concerning topics of interest to directors, meetings with key management and visits to Company facilities.

Board Committees

The Board has established the following committees to assist the Board in discharging its responsibilities: the Audit Committee; the Compensation and Human Resources Committee; the Corporate Governance Committee; and the Compliance and Risk Committee. The Board may from time to time modify any of these Committees or establish new Committees.

The composition, responsibilities and other attributes of each Committee shall be specified in a Charter that shall be adopted by such Committee and approved by the Board. The Charters provide that each Committee will annually evaluate its performance.

Upon the recommendation of the Corporate Governance Committee, the Board of Directors shall appoint the Chairs and members of the Committees, each of whom shall serve at the discretion of the Board. In designating members of the Committees, the Board shall consider the extent to which Committee assignments should be rotated from time to time. While rotating Committee members should be considered periodically, the Board does not believe rotation should be mandated as a policy since there are significant benefits attributable to continuity, experience gained in service on particular committees and utilizing most effectively the individual talents of the directors.

The frequency, length and agenda of meetings of each Committee are determined by the Chair of the Committee, who may consult with members of the Committee and appropriate officers of the Company. Board members who are not members of a particular Committee are welcome to attend meetings of that Committee.

Each Committee's duties may be described briefly as follows:

- *Audit Committee*. The Audit Committee's general purpose is to assist the Board in fulfilling its oversight responsibilities with respect to (1) the audits of Company's financial statements and the integrity of the Company's financial statements and internal controls; (2) the qualifications and independence of the Company's independent auditor (including the Committee's direct responsibility for the engagement of the independent auditor); (3) the performance of the Company's internal audit function and independent auditor; (4) the Company's accounting and financial reporting processes; and (5) the activity of the Company's internal control function, including reviewing decisions with respect to scope, risk assessment, testing plans, and organizational structure.

- *Compensation and Human Resources Committee*. The Compensation and Human Resources Committee's general purpose is to assist the Board in fulfilling its responsibilities with respect to executive compensation and human resources matters, including (1) reviewing and approving corporate goals and objectives relevant to the compensation of the CEO; in coordination with the Corporate Governance Committee, evaluating his or her performance in light of those goals and objectives; and determining and approving his or her compensation based upon such evaluation; and (2) determining the compensation of senior executives other than the CEO, including determinations regarding equity-based and other incentive compensation awards.

- *Corporate Governance Committee.* The Corporate Governance Committee's general purpose is to assist the Board in fulfilling its responsibilities with respect to the governance of the Company, and includes making recommendations to the Board concerning (1) the size and composition of the Board, the qualifications and independence of the directors, and the recruitment and selection of individuals to stand for election as directors; (2) the organization and operation of the Board, including the nature, size and composition of Committees, the designation of Committee Chairs, the designation of a Lead Independent Director, Chairman of the Board or similar position, and the process for distribution of information to the Board and its Committees; and (3) the compensation of non-employee directors.

- *Compliance and Risk Committee.* The Compliance and Risk Committee's general purposes are (i) to provide general oversight to the Company's Risk and Compliance functions; (ii) to provide input to management in the identification, assessment and mitigation of enterprise-wide risks faced by the Company both internally and externally; and (iii) to provide recommendations to the Board with respect to its review of the Company's business practices and compliance activities and enterprise risk management.

It is the policy of the Board that all of the members of the Audit Committee, the Compensation and Human Resources Committee and the Corporate Governance Committee will be independent directors.

Communications with Stockholders and Other Interested Parties

The Board is interested in receiving communications from stockholders and other interested parties, which would include customers, suppliers and employees. Such parties may contact any member (or members) of the Board or any Committee, the non-employee directors as a group, or the Chair of any committee, by mail or electronically. In addition, the Audit Committee is interested in receiving communications from employees and other interested parties, which would include stockholders, customers and suppliers, on issues regarding accounting, internal accounting controls or auditing matters. Any such correspondence should be addressed to the appropriate person or persons, either by name or title, and sent by regular mail to the office of the Corporate Secretary at One CA Plaza, Islandia, New York 11749, or by e-mail to directors@ca.com.

The Board has determined that the following types of communications are not related to the duties and responsibilities of the Board and its committees and are, therefore, not appropriate: spam and similar junk mail and mass mailings; product complaints, product inquiries and new product suggestions; résumés and other job inquiries; surveys; business solicitations or advertisements; and any communication that is unduly hostile, threatening, illegal or similarly unsuitable. Each communication received as described above will be forwarded to the directors, unless the Corporate Secretary determines said communication is not appropriate. Regardless, certain of these communications will be forwarded to others in the Company for review and action, when appropriate, or to the directors upon request.

Management Development and Succession Planning

The Board, with recommendations from the Corporate Governance Committee and the Compensation and Human Resources Committee, shall approve and maintain a succession plan for the CEO. On an annual basis, the Corporate Governance Committee and the Compensation and Human Resources Committee shall present to the Board a report on succession planning for senior management and a report on management development.

Executive Stock Ownership Guidelines

Executive stock ownership guidelines have been adopted under which all members of the Senior Leadership Team must achieve ownership thresholds based on a multiple of their base salary.

These Principles

These Principles shall be subject to review, at least annually, by the Board or the Corporate Governance Committee, and any changes deemed appropriate shall be adopted by the Board, on the recommendation of the Corporate Governance Committee.

Compliance and Risk Committee Charter of CA, Inc.

General

The purpose of this **Charter** is to set forth the composition, authority and responsibilities of the Compliance and Risk Committee (the "Committee") of the Board of Directors of CA, Inc. (the "Company").

Composition

The members of the Committee are designated by the Board, on the recommendation of the Corporate Governance Committee of the Board, in accordance with the Company's By-laws, and serve at the discretion of the Board. The Board appoints one member of the Committee as Chair of the Committee.

Authority and Responsibilities

General. The general purposes of the Committee are (i) to provide general oversight to the Company's Risk and Compliance functions; (ii) to provide input to management in the identification, assessment and mitigation of enterprise-wide risks faced by the Company both internally and externally; and (iii) to provide recommendations to the Board with respect to its review of the Company's business practices and compliance activities and enterprise risk management. The Executive Vice President, Risk and Chief Administrative Officer shall report functionally to the Committee with respect to the Company's Enterprise Risk Management function, and the Executive Vice President and General Counsel shall report functionally to the Committee with respect to the Company's Business Practices and Compliance function, as well as to the Chief Executive Officer; provided, however, that the Executive Vice President, Risk and Chief Administrative Officer, the Executive Vice President and General Counsel, the Chief Compliance Officer, the Chief Ethics Officer and the Chief Risk Officer will at all times have unrestricted access to the Committee or any member of the Committee or the Board for any purpose he or she deems appropriate.

Business Practices and Compliance Oversight Responsibilities. The Committee will assist the Board in fulfilling its oversight responsibilities with respect to the Company's compliance with legal and regulatory requirements. In particular, the Committee will:

1. Oversee the activities of the Business Practices and Compliance functions. The Company's Chief Compliance Officer and the Company's Chief Ethics Officer will report directly to the Committee and to the Company's Executive Vice President and General Counsel (unless the Chief Compliance Officer or the Chief Ethics Officer is also the Executive Vice President and General Counsel).

2. Review with the Audit Committee of the Board on a timely basis all matters, including complaints and risks, relating to accounting and financial reporting matters.

3. Oversee the adoption and maintenance of procedures to ensure that all inquiries raised by governmental entities, or by stockholders, customers, suppliers and employees, regarding compliance and ethics matters receive prompt review by or under the authority of the Chief Compliance Officer or the Chief Ethics Officer, including, as appropriate, the reporting of such matters to the Committee and the Board.

4. Oversee the establishment and maintenance of a comprehensive compliance and ethics program, including an ethics and compliance training program for all employees, designed to minimize the possibility of violations of the federal securities and other laws by the Company.

5. Oversee the establishment and maintenance of a written plan designed to ensure the improvement and ongoing effectiveness of communications with all governmental agencies engaged in inquiries or investigations of the Company, which plan will provide for: (a) regular reporting by management and outside and internal counsel to the Committee and, as appropriate, the Board regarding communications with those governmental agencies, including providing to the Committee copies of all written communications to and from those agencies; (b) complete and prompt access for those agencies to the Company and its management; (c) meetings between those agencies and the Board or its committees, upon the request of those agencies; and (d) employee training designed to improve communication and cooperation with those agencies.

6. Monitor the process for communicating to employees the Company's Code of Conduct and the importance of compliance therewith, including: (a) the maintenance and periodic review of the Code; and (b) assuring employees that no retaliation or other negative action will be taken against any employee because he or she submits any report or complaint concerning potential violations of law or other misconduct and concerns regarding accounting, auditing or internal control matters.

Enterprise Risk Management Oversight Responsibilities. The Committee will assist the Board in fulfilling its oversight responsibilities with respect to assessing major risks facing the Company and considering strategies for their management and mitigation. In particular, the Committee will:

1.   Review with management, including the Executive Vice President, Risk and Chief Administrative Officer and the Chief Risk Officer, the significant risks, trends and uncertainties arising with respect to the Company's strategies, business operations, financial reporting, and legal and regulatory affairs, and provide input and guidance on the Company's risk tolerances.

2.   Review with management, including the Executive Vice President, Risk and Chief Administrative Officer and the Chief Risk Officer, the Company's major risk exposures and the steps management has taken to identify, control and monitor such exposures, including guidelines and policies to govern the process by which risk assessment and risk management are undertaken.

The Company's Chief Risk Officer will report directly to the Committee and to the Company's Executive Vice President, Risk and Chief Administrative Officer (unless the Chief Risk Officer is also the Executive Vice President, Risk and Chief Administrative Officer).

Proxy Statement Report. The Committee may consider rendering (but is not required to render) a report on the Committee'sactivities and achievements for inclusion in the Company's proxy statements.

Delegation of Authority

The Committee may delegate authority to one or more members or subcommittees when deemed appropriate, provided that the actions of any such members or subcommittees are reported to the full Committee no later than at its next scheduled meeting.

Counsel and Other Delegation of Authority; Company Funding Obligations

The Committee has the authority, to the extent it deems necessary or appropriate, to retain and terminate the retention of independent legal counsel, or other advisors, to assist the Committee in carrying out its responsibilities. The Company will provide for appropriate funding, as determined by the Committee, to pay any such counsel or other advisors retained by the Committee and to pay ordinary administrative expenses of the Committee that are necessary or appropriate in carrying out its duties.

Meetings; Executive Sessions

The Committee meets as often as it deems necessary. The Committee meets periodically in executive sessions, with or without such officers or other employees of the Company, counsel to the Company, counsel or other advisors to the Committee, or other parties, as the Committee may determine. Meeting agendas will be prepared and provided in advance to the Committee, together with appropriate briefing materials.

Reports to the Board; Minutes

The Committee will make regular reports to the Board regarding the Committee's activities and will make reports to the Company's Audit Committee from time to time, as appropriate. Minutes of the meetings and other actions of the Committee will be prepared and submitted for approval by the Committee and will be furnished to the Board at regular intervals.

Committee Self-Assessment

The Committee will conduct an annual self-assessment of its performance with respect to its purposes and the authority and responsibilities set forth in this Charter. The results of the self-assessment will be reported to the Board.

Committee Charter

This Charter will be subject to review and approval by the Board. The Committee will review this Charter annually and adopt any changes deemed appropriate, subject to approval by the Board.

Index

Numbers

2003 Blackout, 125

A

accountability, 19, 101, 165
adjustable-rate mortgages
  (ARMs), 22
anomaly detection, 130
Audit Committee, 62
authority levels, setting, 19

B

Barings Bank, 18
best practices, lending, 22
Board of Directors
    best practices, 59
    evolution of, 58
    financial crisis and, 56
     governance and, 56
    utilizing experience of, 60
brand enhancement, 186
business objectives, 26
business requirements,
    identifying, 26

C

Capability Maturity Model
  Integration (CMMI), 94, 95
carbon footprints, 186, 190, 191,
  192, 195, 196, 202
carbon trading, 199
CEO, role of, 59
Chairman of the Board, role of, 59
change and configuration
  management, 91
Chief Compliance Officer (CCO), 89
Chief Information Officer (CIO),
  89, 91
Chief Risk Officer, 57, 58, 65, 66,
  67, 68
cloud computing, 174
Code of Conduct, 69
collateralized debt obligations
  (CDOs), 23
collateralized debt organizations
  (CDOs), 67
Committee of Sponsoring
  Organizations (COSO), 9, 78, 128
committees, 61
community-based resources, 192
Compensation and Human
  Resources Committee, 63

compliance, 69, 104, 162
Compliance and Risk Committee, 58, 62, 63, 64, 65, 66, 67, 68
compliance audits, 92
compliance controls, 32
compliance information, centralizing, 138
compliance management, automating, 137
compliance tracking, 144
compliance, defined, 16
consumption reduction, 186
control objectives, 29
Control Objectives for Information and Related Technology (COBIT), 129
Control Objectives for IT (COBIT), 92
controls
    automation, 96
    maturity, 94
    rationalization of, 98
corporate governance, 3, 9, 158
Corporate Governance Committee, 63
corporate policies, setting, 19
corrective controls, 30
cost reduction, 118
cost savings, 186
customer value, 116

D

dashboards, 140
Data Encryption Standard encryption (3DES), 33
Deferred Prosecution Agreement (DPA), 57
detective controls, 30
directing vs. managing, 60

disaster recovery, 92

E

Ecomagination campaign, 186
economic resources, 192
ecoSoftware, 187, 189, 194, 200
eDiscovery, 159, 160, 161, 166, 169, 170, 171, 173, 177, 180
Eich, Kelly, 132
Electronically Stored Information (ESI), 170, 177, 178
Email archiving, 160
Enron, 17, 58
enterprise resource planning (ERP) systems, 151, 152
enterprise risk, 26
Enterprise Risk Management (ERM), 3, 78, 80, 83
Environmental Protection Agency (EPA), 195, 200, 201, 204
environmental resource group, 192
European Union (EU), 9, 136
experience, as catalyst for change, 57

F

Fannie Mae, 23
Federal Sentencing Guidelines, 74
Federated Records Management (FRM), 160, 162, 167
finance, challenges and opportunities, 155
finance, evolution of, 145
finance, goals, 148
finance, governance and, 147
finance, interdependencies, 146
finance, intersections of processes, 148
finance, role of, 144

finance, streamlining, 153
finance, technology and, 150
finance, traditional, 145
finance, transparency, 149
financial GRC, 3
Financial Industry Regulatory
  Authority (FINRA), 162, 179
flexibility, 137
Foreign Corrupt Practices Act
  (FCPA), 73, 84
formality, 3, 12
Freddie Mac, 23
Freedom of Information Act, 160

G

General Electric (GE), 186
generally accepted accounting
  principles (GAAP), 152
Global Crossing, 6, 17
globalization, 9
governance
    defined, 2, 16
    goals of, 17
    real world examples, 21
    responsibilities of, 25
    stakeholders, 19
    sustainability and, 189, 199
governance, risk, and compliance
  (GRC), 3, 15, 16, 76, 77, 78, 79,
  80, 81, 82, 84, 85
Gramm-Leach-Bliley Act (GLBA), 8
Greenhouse Gas Protocol (GHG
  Protocol), 196, 197
greenwashing, 186

H

Health Insurance Portability and
  Accountability Act (HIPAA), 7,
  82, 83, 128, 129, 132, 133, 138,
  162, 179
housing bubble, 1
human resources, 113

I

identity and access management, 91
impact, 102
increased user productivity, 118
Information Governance (IG),
    157, 159, 162, 163, 165, 166,
    167, 168, 169, 170, 171, 173,
    178, 180
    basics of, 158
    benefits, 167
    cloud computing and, 174
    components, 159
    discovery and, 170
    driving forces for, 164
    framework, 175
    getting started, 179
    goals, 163
    IT and, 172
    objectives, 159
    social implications of, 166
    steps to achieving, 176
information management, 91
information security, 158
information silos, 10
Information Systems Audit and
  Control Association (ISACA), 92
information, defined, 158
innovation, 166
interest rates, 1
International Financial Reporting
  Standards (IFRS), 152, 153
International Organization of
  Standardization (ISO), 9

International Organization of
Standards (ISO), 93, 94
ISO 20000, 94
ISO/IEC 38500:2008 standard, 176
IT Compliance Group, 87, 88, 89,
  90, 101, 105, 106
IT Compliance Officer, 88, 89, 90,
  100, 104
IT GRC, 4, 92
IT Project Life Cycle, 91
IT
    compliance controls, 91
    GRC and, 88
    risk vs. cost, 90
    sustainability and, 203

K

Key Performance Indicators
  (KPIs), 115, 190
key risk indicators (KRIs), 102
Kotter, John P., 70

L

Leeson, Nick, 18
lights on requests, 111
likelihood, 102

M

Madoff, Bernard, 165, 166
monitoring and reporting, 81

N

National Institute of Standards
  and Technology (NIST), 92
New Deal, 5

North American Electric
  Reliability Corporation (NERC),
  125

O

Obama, Barack, 165, 172
operational controls, 94
operational governance, 3
operations management, 92
orphan accounts, 31
oversight, 19

P

Payment Card Industry (PCI), 82
Payment Card Industry Data
  Security Standard (PCI DSS), 7,
  26, 33
policies
    creating, 26
    life cycle, 27, 33
    management of, 27
    review of, 28
portfolio management, 109, 110,
  111, 114, 116, 117, 119
prescriptive approach, regulation,
  128
preventative controls, 30
principle-based approach,
  regulation, 128
principle-based regulations, 153
proactive control design, 94
Project and Portfolio Management
  (PPM), 107, 108, 109, 110, 112,
  114, 115, 116, 117, 119, 121
Project Management Body of
  Knowledge (PMBOK), 120

R

regulation, 2, 6, 8, 9, 10
  approaches to, 127
  awareness, 131
  model, 129
  transnational, 136
regulatory compliance, 131
regulatory process, 134
regulatory requirements, 26
return on investment (ROI), 117
revenue generation, 187
revenue increase, 118
rigor, 3, 12
risk framework, 67
risk management, defined, 16
risk management, key failures of, 23
risk metrics, defining, 101
risk, defined, 16
risk, integrated approach to, 80
round-trip management, 21
rule-based regulations, 153

S

Sarbanes-Oxley Act (SOX), 5, 6,
  7, 8, 9, 10, 11, 18, 70, 74, 76, 82,
  83, 84, 89, 94, 98, 105, 126, 128,
  129, 133, 137, 138, 162, 179
security, information, 165
segregation of duties (SOD), 30, 91
software development life cycle
  (SDLC), 91
Stage-Gate, 119

Standard & Poor's, 135
subprime-mortgage crisis, 2
sustainability
  alignment factors, 185, 194
  building program for, 189
  explained, 183
  governance and, 189, 199
  investing in, 188
  IT and, 203
systematizing governance, 151

T

tax management, 145
threat management, 91
transparency, 3, 5, 6, 7, 12, 135,
  144, 165
transparency, creating, 17
Treadway Commission, 9

U

U.S. Federal Energy Regulatory
  Commission (FERC), 125, 126
Unified Compliance Framework
  (UCF), 98, 138
unified governance approach, 11

V

value, 17, 144
vulnerability management, 91

W

WorldCom, 58

You Need the Companion eBook

Your purchase of this book entitles you to buy the companion PDF-version eBook for only $10. Take the weightless companion with you anywhere.

We believe this Apress title will prove so indispensable that you'll want to carry it with you everywhere, which is why we are offering the companion eBook (in PDF format) for $10 to customers who purchase this book now. Convenient and fully searchable, the PDF version of any content-rich, page-heavy Apress book makes a valuable addition to your programming library. You can easily find and copy code—or perform examples by quickly toggling between instructions and the application. Even simultaneously tackling a donut, diet soda, and complex code becomes simplified with hands-free eBooks!

Once you purchase your book, getting the $10 companion eBook is simple:

❶ Visit **www.apress.com/promo/tendollars/**.

❷ Complete a basic registration form to receive a randomly generated question about this title.

❸ Answer the question correctly in 60 seconds, and you will receive a promotional code to redeem for the $10.00 eBook.

THE EXPERT'S VOICE™

233 Spring Street, New York, NY 10013

All Apress eBooks subject to copyright protection. No part may be reproduced or transmitted in any form or by any means, electronic or mechanical, including photocopying, recording, or by any information storage or retrieval system, without the prior written permission of the copyright owner and the publisher. The purchaser may print the work in full or in part for their own noncommercial use. The purchaser may place the eBook title on any of their personal computers for their own personal reading and reference.

Offer valid through 4/10.